OMA - Rem Koolhaas

Jacques Lucan

OMA - Rem Koolhaas

Architecture 1970–1990

Princeton Architectural Press

Published by
Princeton Architectural Press
37 East 7th Street
New York, NY 10003
212.995.9620
ISBN 1-878271-55-5

Production Editor
David Block
English translations by
David Block
Stefanie Lew
Kevin C. Lippert
Lois Nesbitt
Marguerite McGoldrick
Antony Shugaar
Book design
Ken Botnick and Kevin C. Lippert
Thanks to
Sheila Cohen, Scott Corbin, Antje Fritsch,
Clare Jacobson, Ann C. Urban, Ellen
McGoldrick, and Ann Parham

Library of Congress Catologuing in
Publication Data is available from
the publisher

Contents

Foreword

More than ten years ago, in 1978, Rem Koolhaas made himself known with a now out-of-print book, *Delirious New York*, a paradoxical work that told the history of a "theoretical" Manhattan at the same time that it proposed a method for investigating architecture and urbanism, a plan for a "culture of congestion" in which the exploitation of a programmatic density was recognized as a fundamental condition of the contemporary metropolis.

Under the mysterious acronym OMA (Office for Metropolitan Architecture), Elia and Zoe Zenghelis, Rem Koolhaas, and Madelon Vriesendorp signed their projects and provocative images.

In 1980, Rem Koolhaas opened an OMA office in Rotterdam, the largest port and industrial city in Holland; it is the projects and built works of the last decade that are shown in the following pages, with a special section on the most recent works (1989–91).

This book does not, however, trace the complete works of Rem Koolhaas. The choice of projects responds to two objectives.

The first is to publish works that synthesize OMA's unique mode of thinking by showing all the iconographic elements indispensable to its understanding, accompanied by explanatory texts by the architects in order to prevent superficial interpretations of the projects.

The second is to establish connections in the series of projects which develop the architectural and urbanistic themes that are constant across different programs and sites, to extract the rationality and coherence of their work.

These choices also mean that we are obliged to move beyond a fascination with seductive images. Rem Koolhaas continues to create propositions that bear untiringly against the settled prejudices of theory. Each project is defined by the logical order of purpose, which is not to say that this coherence is not subject to inflections or revisions or that it does not produce some surprises. The work of Rem Koolhaas encompasses the steps towards understanding the phenomena of the contemporary metropolis in such a way as to elicit responses to the programs that are proposed to him.

In the end, for Rem Koolhaas, the architect is obliged to confront the chaos of the metropolis with the knowledge that his "reforming" action is nothing more than a precarious resistance. The difficulty of any postion resides in this radical uncertainty, which only feeds on optimism, that of always wanting to take up again "the true fire of modernity," offering a foundation for the programs of the future.   *J.L.*

Exodus, or the Voluntary Prisoners of Architecture, 1972

The Rational Rebel, or the Urban Agenda of OMA

Jean-Louis Cohen

Serene provocator, silent dynamiter, Rem Koolhaas has worked for fifteen years as an extraordinary commentator on the condition of late twentieth century cities. His inquiries can take the classic form of a book, or with certain of the less conventional ones, a project, but in all cases they reveal, more often than not, the fashions, the forgotten or neglected dimensions of the large contemporary city.

With the dexterity of a surgeon, but without so much of the vaunted corporate sponsorship employed by twentieth-century planners, Koolhaas probes and cuts at the sources of urban blight. His tour of the world first led him to take seriously the Berlin wall, the destiny of which he has been investigating—contrary to fashion—since 1972, anticipating the questions raised by the sudden obsolescence of a fortification gradually dismantled since autumn 1989. With the same ferocity for received ideas, he is exploring today the unforeseeable agglomerations of modern Asia, though not without passing through several cities of the United States and Western Europe, following a logic grounded in, or more often, ricocheting off the objective hazards of professional life.

A fantastic history of modern cities

Koolhaas's urban projects thus simultaneously stem from their own initiatives and from precise, localized directives, which he treats with utmost respect while nonetheless inflecting them and holding them up to derision. Responding to these two sets of demands, the order of the analysis converges with the order of the conception. And if the explicitly historical projects in *Delirious New York* harkened back in 1978 in their "fiction-conclusion" to specific architectural strategies, the 1980 project for Kochstraße in Berlin rests, inversely, on actual historic projects in the center city initiated to form a reference perimeter beyond the boundary of the competition site. Framed in distinct sequences, the metropolitan observation that OMA proposes constitutes a sort of history of the fantastic. Surprising in its content—consisting of a collage of heterogenous projects—this history is especially startling because of the staging it proposes for these episodes, placing them in unforeseeable scenarios. The history of urban strategies employed in Rem Koolhaas's projects is grounded in the notion of *retroaction*, as presented in *Delirious New York: A Retroactive Manifesto for Manhattan*. Constructed in part with the existing body of architectural projects, but also with the attitudes of avant-garde Europeans regarding Manhattan, Koolhaas's retroactive position has become more and more complex in its ulterior conjectural manipulations. It no longer acts solely to reconstruct and to order, in an almost fictive manner, the succession of commentaries and projects making up a given city. Rem Koolhaas measures and slices the body of architectural history with his retroactive scissors. He transforms, by detaching them from their contexts, the grand simplifying paradigms which characterize certain projects of the German *neues Bauen* or the Russian Constructivists into complex and pertinent structural agendas. This operation of "decontextualization" makes units comprising an explanatory scale out of these typological or territorial principles, with whose aid it becomes possible to measure the impact of contemporary projects. The preliminary studies for the project at IJ-

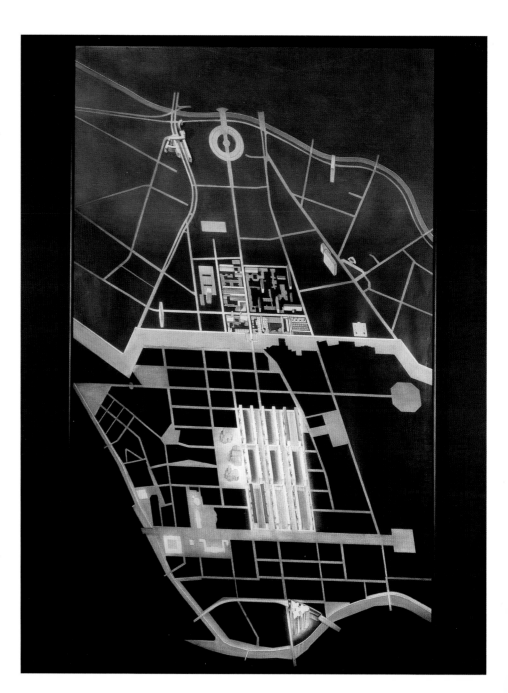

plein in Amsterdam is thus grounded in the free manipulation of morphological principles inferred from a dozen seminal projects of European functionalism. With this game of mirrors, Koolhaas pays homage, of a sort, to the experimental dimension of projects hitherto relegated to history—a dimension highly acclaimed at the time of their elaboration[1]—and gives them new operational pertinence, using them as more than historical background.

No longer applied solely to a precise urban framework like Manhattan or Berlin, this retroactive principle regulates Koolhaas's paradoxical use of a history which more often than not encompasses only a closed circle of heroes and episodes. It is not simply a question of a manipulation of the architectural forms of the great moderns, similar to the practice of the mannerists of today, when they use for instrumental ends the pilotis and the strip windows of Le Corbusier or the girders of the constructivists. For his part, Koolhaas is interested in the structuring potential of territorial projects or certain monumental themes of the "Modern Movement." Taking seriously the paradigmatic dimension of the plans for the city-gardens and for the *Siedlungen* as extensions of the great metropolitan plans proposed by functionalist culture, he subjects these structures to fragmentation and ground densification in the crucible of present urban structure, coolly observing the result of unforeseeable chemical reactions. Several clear fixations with regard to these sparingly defined themes appear in this thinking. The first pertains to Russian Constructivism and its premier member, the child prodigy Ivan Leonidov. For several years (starting in 1974), Koolhaas devoted himself to exhuming, in collaboration with the Dutch historian Gerrit Oorthuys, the belated—and heavily symbolically charged—project for the three-level skyscraper Leonidov sketched for the Commisioner of Heavy Industrial Workers in 1934.[2] But the promised monograph did not appear, and Koolhaas turned his attention to the ordering mechanisms Leonidov elaborated in his 1930 polemics on "disurbanism," especially in the linear project imagined for the new town of Magnitogorsk.[3] If Leonidov's territorial grid was destined to be referenced fairly often in OMA's projects, the method of codification or, more often, notation of ideas used by the Russian architect was also not neglected. A recourse to sometimes childish pictograms allowing for the representation in plan of the theoretical spatial disposition of a given activity figured heavily in 1982 for the project of the Parc de la Villette—with substantial relevance, since the uses proposed for that space were, at the time of the competition, virtual. Beyond any graphic or pictorial game, so important in the common work of the two architect/painter couples who founded OMA, comprising Rem Koolhaas and Madelon Vriesendorp, the first couple, and Elias and Zoé Zenghelis, the second couple, the process reinforces not the rigor of *representation*, but the rigor of the urban agenda. Broadacre City, conceived by Frank Lloyd Wright in 1934, was another great antiurbanist project practically contemporary with the work of Leonidov, but founded on sociological premises and absolutely opposite technology; Koolhaas sees it as the only paradigm as yet exploitable by the American urban culture of this century. Wright's

evocation, which contains, according to Koolhaas, "the best expression of the ineluctable disorder with which we must live,"[4] corresponds to a redeployment of OMA's work toward suburban or completely nonurban sites, such as the island of Antiparos, for which a parcelization project was elaborated in 1981. In these urban-fabric projects—the term does not imply that they were developed on flat terrain—the patchwork of parcels and the regularly-planted houses of Broadacre City, homologous but differentiated, are primary. OMA employs a third reference for the territorial or urban fragmentation: Mies van der Rohe's virtuosity in planting vertical partitioning in the ground often shows through. Here, no longer is the utopian of the Friedrichstraße skyscraper or the builder of the Seagram Building at work, but rather it is Mies as the indefatigable arranger of corridors and patios between the brick villa of 1924 and the Resor house of 1940.[5] The "Miesian" repertoire is delightfully employed by OMA—since it allows precise carving of buildings through partitioning large volumes or through translating identical distributions—but also to regulate within a unique form the coexistence of small closed spaces and large open spaces.
The references advanced by OMA are, however, far from limiting themselves to the groundbreaking planning and architecture projects or to the period between the wars; they sweep over a wide spectrum consisting of the impressions Rem Koolhaas gathers on his weekly flights over the rural Dutch countryside whose crosshatched pattern of canals and fields thickly blanketed with greenhouses[6] recall the Roman *centuriato*.
The presence of Roman settlements affirms

every so often the unexpected form of certain urban reconstruction projects: the rehabilitation plan for Bijlmermeer doubtless more closely resembles the the Roman forum, used as an example of an assemblage of public open spaces, than the agricultural parcels of the Emilian plain. OMA's involvement with the rehabilitation of the urban layout of Bijlmermeer, whose vast tracts to the south of Amsterdam constitute one of the least complex products of postwar state-supported functionalism, is the occasion for a reconsideration of the famous hexagonal frame so dear to the architects of Team X. That this palimpsest does not in the meantime dissimulate the persistence of certain major themes developed in the work of Jakob Bakema, Aldo Van Eyck, or other founders of a last-gasp group of CIAM insiders, whose ideas are "apparently completely *dépassé* when judged formally" has, for Rem Koolhaas, "very precisely accented the problems that arose in their time."[7] Even more than the kinship of architectural writing to the functionalists, noted by Stanislaus von Moos,[8] Koolhaas employs the techniques of global reasoning used in the realm of Dutch architecture by the last generation of CIAM, their care for the functional relationships between buildings and fractions of cities, and occasionally, their techniques of graphic notation. Starting before *Delirious New York*, Rem Koolhaas thus constructed an imaginary museum to which certain flagrant injustices of orthodox history were banished. When he pays homage to Wallace Harrison, stigmatised the past few decades for having "stolen" from Le Corbusier the chairmanship of the United Nations committee, or when he deigns to take into account, and

Top

IJ-Plein, Amsterdam, 1980–1989, studies of
several modern projects inscribed on the site

Bottom

OMA's completed project

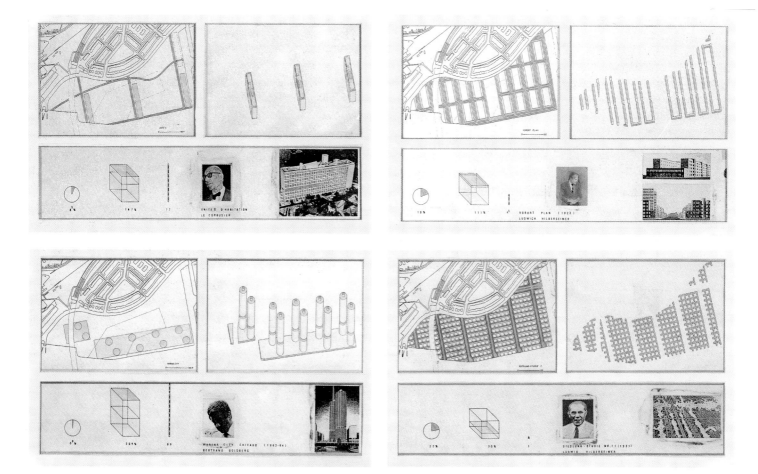

occasionally praise, the work of certain commercial Atlanta firms, Koolhaas takes a rare liberty in a modern architecture restricted to a tight circle of high priests.

But OMA's method is not based so much on citation, and the rows of ideal buildings aligned on Manhattan's grid in *Delirious New York* are not offerings of a supermarket of architectural themes. The assemblage of projects exhumed by Koolhaas has nothing like a *Città analoga* or a *Collage City*. Where Aldo Rossi perpetuates the permanences and the immobile identity of *locus*, where Colin Rowe revels in the superposition of baroque figures, there remains for OMA to exploit the cumulative experience of the laboratory of modern architecture to define the rules for combining functions and surfaces. Territorial plans, urban projects, or fragments of collected space thus assemble themselves to constitute a system of units similar to that which plagued the scientific world before the advent of a strategy of unification which allowed the comparison of measurements of distance, radioactivity, and even electrical resistance. If it is to allow measurement, this system can in no way be a simple toolbox or a stock of isolated forms. In "The City of the Captive Globe," Koolhaas's architectural references rested stiffly on their pedestals, waiting for a signal. With the preoccupation with connections and interrelations common to OMA's recent urban projects, these references constitute even now the basis for a system of open measurement.

Function and fabric, or the band city

We must not be deceived by the supple lines enveloping OMA's projects. They are grounded not in an existing formal order on which functions are distributed, but on an extremely precise accounting of the programmatic expectations of the institutions sponsoring the competitions. Rem Koolhaas takes the programs seriously, from the most puerile to the most pompous, and relies on them explicitly, giving free reign to their internal contradictions, however destructive they may be.

Constrained by the mass of programmatic requirements for the Parc de la Villette (1982), the OMA team worked with the internal equilibria of the document—equilibria doubtlessly unrecognized by certain of its authors—to elaborate a structure grounded in the frequencies of the different activities and their interrelationships. This approach can be seen as relevant to a minor branch of a functionalism too soon judged moribund, in that it rests on the idea of a grid so dear to CIAM. But functionalist classification systems are distorted by this approach in a manner both ironic and cruel.

A rigid matrix serving to support the comparative work CIAM did on the "functional city" for the Congress of Athens—a mechanism again consolidated for the postwar congress at the instigation of Le Corbusier, who sought a proving ground for the *Modulor*—the grid was a mechanism which allowed control over the orthodoxy of the development of European cities, reducing topological, morphological, and social differences to graphic scribbles. It was in some sense the instrument of a unifying retroaction, prelude to a projected homogenization which will never take place, inasmuch as the differences between the passengers on the *Patris II* were too great.[9]

The grids OMA uses, from La Villette to Melun-Sénart, permit the construction of a

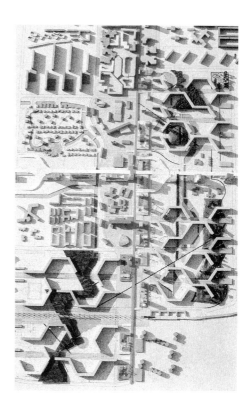

project laden with double meaning pertaining both to the location of territorial regularities—contours, primary grids, infrastructure—and to the identification of programmatic regularities—repetitive spaces, services, poles of intensity, etc. Thus they sanction the recognition of an existing spatial order, constituted in the solidification of lines (and functions, as well), and the recognition of a new social order, stemming from a process of inquiry and conjecture, very scrupulously taken into account by the architects. Exploring the potentials of the program sometimes entails, voluntarily or not, their implosion under the pressure of their internal condradictions. Under the grave regard of Rem Koolhaas, the functional incompatibilities or oppositions are placed in relief and thrown into collision, casting doubt on the coherence of the program and destabilizing the very foundations on which the procedure of program writing rests. Based upon an austere, transparent interpretation of the initial programmatic interpretations, the horizontal swaths of OMA's great urban projects effect a territorial conquest in which the tradition of the polder is equally represented with CIAM's. In their mastery of parsimoniously apportioned territory these swaths contain, like the disurbanist systems of 1930 or like Broadacre City, a potential for unlimited growth; they integrate themselves into a *Ranstad* (the Dutch conurbation) less imaginary than one would think.

OMA's swaths define a principle of functional distribution and a sometimes implicit fundamental principle of parcelization, and they contribute to the rules for the disposition of urban and architectural objects. But it is a long way from the free space of the

Charter of Athens, that "anti-idea of the city" which Bernard Huet stigmatized,[10] to OMA's spaces saturated with lines and intentions, which allow both for the play of chance elements and for formal interventions, according to configurations deduced not from theory, but from the observation of large cities, whose transformation is still being completed in the twentieth century. Primary lines of force, the functional matrices deployed in the initial phase of OMA's conjectural work only take on a material presence when they acquire depth, when they become constructed forms. This transmutation intervenes through the mobilization of a repertoire of territorial and architectural forms which offer not only conceptual options, but also means of conjugation and of formal composition among them. With this operation, OMA distances itself both from conventional solutions of the first functionalists and the lines of traditional landscape painters. In the first place, grounded in the repetition of so-called optimal functional units, it opposes a dangerous plurality, one justified by the dissymmetries of the programs; secondly, grounded in the use of axes, which Koolhaas justly characterizes as a "*maladie française*," it opposes the principle of the band. These bands can be defined, according to the scale at which they are considered, as linear systems endowed with a certain depth or as quadrilaterals laterally expanded along one of their dimensions. They are also succeptible to being perceived as arising from the the deconstruction of continuous urban structures—Manhattan's grid can be read as a juxtaposition of bands, stemming as much from a crossing of parallel roads as from a carving-up of agricultural fields.

In the project for the Parc de la Villette, where the band principle finds its first formulation, the band is legitimized by programmatic fragmentation into surfaces and by the combination of these surfaces (directed by an algorithm of spatial allocation from the 1960s). In more recent projects, the bands have acquired a different significance, less linearly determined by the fragmentation of uses. As proving grounds for the practical utopias of La Villette, they define the great transversals woven into the project for Bijlmermeer, proposing a new compartmentalization and a new reading for the petrified sinusoids of existing constructions. In the project for Melun-Sénart, the game is both richer and more complex, since the bands correspond, on the one hand, to the physical conditions of the site (comprising large existing infrastructure or the edge of the site across from the forest), and on the other hand, to systems of urban fragmentation leading to particular building types—islands or autonomous buildings. Another modality of Rem Koolhaas's rapport with functionalism appears here. Where the great projects by the founders of CIAM essentially constructed a superposition of figures (buildings) on a background ("free" space, isotropic and homogenous with the "functional" city), OMA's projects tend to superimpose a new, functional background, on the geographic one; then, in a second operation is added a third background, on which the network of figures appears as a diffused ensemble. Far from resolving to a simply binary relationship between figure and ground, the identity of each building results from an integration of its coordinates in the network of bands and from its own functional and symbolic deter-

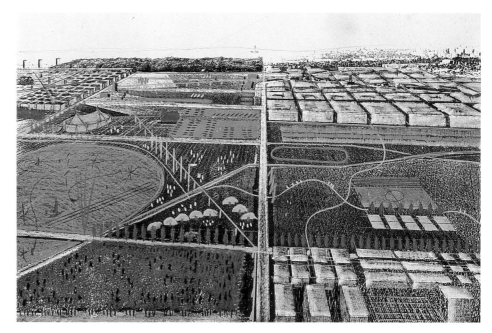

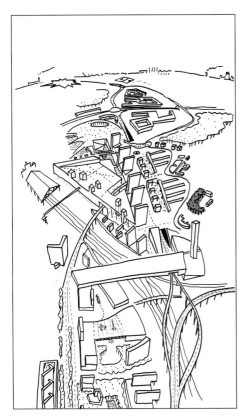

minations.

Is this to say that all concept for composition has disappeared from these projects and that the idea of composition has ceased to operate? This is not at all the case. Rejection of the axis does not imply rejection of the alignment. Disdain for imitating clichés of the Modern movement does not imply a part and parcel rejection of its solutions. Certain configurations can thus rest on the principles explored around 1929 by Leonidov or Ernst May, but only by subverting them in favor of the outline or the form of the buildings. In this manner the massing plan for IJ-plein explored the potential of rows,[11] while that for Melun-Sénart employed the generosity of open spaces used at Magnitogorsk—but in a new, already congested town. Other configurations will, on the other hand, use methods of distribution obtained by collecting fragments of functionalist or constructivist compositions, but on plans arising from other experiences. The IJ-plein complex inserts into a plan of German or Dutch inspiration a constructivist object: the great row OMA constructed reflects more of an inspiration from Ginzburg than from Leonidov; it effectively integrates the mechanisms of Narkomfin's House-commune and the typological principles of the movable houses designed for the disurbanist enterprises.[12]

OMA's pictorial renderings lend the vigor of a stereotype to certain projects, although the violent game of colours and contours in their plans should not deceive. The combination and interpenetration of the spatial sequences are not regulated by painterly principles, taken from the great abstract painters. The methods of assembling spatial components and the method of specifying

nascent architectural programs reveal above all the influence of the cinema, though the framing of sequences in the project for Melun-Sénart hints more at a choreographic notation. Rem Koolhaas's initial vocation as a screenwriter could be found in an architectural fiction like "The City of the Captive Globe," out of which grew *Delirious New York*. The urban projects elaborated in the 1980s followed this route, but manipulated the programs issued by authentic living technocrats. If the screenplay, in this case, is out of OMA's hands, then the cutting, the centering, and, *last but not least*, the editing is up to them. Especially the editing, assembling the successive spatial scenes along the bands, or governing, contrariwise, their superposition. From this point, the foreseeable regularity of the grid gives way to a sequence of bands as unexpected and startling as one assembled from a pile of outtakes on the floor of the editing studio.

The contemporary metropolis: new paradigms

Formulated from contact with New York, the vertical metropolis, or more accurately, from Manhattan, the most vertical *borough* (the image of the city and of the borough often intermingle), the theory of *congestion* takes on another value in suburban systems on which Koolhaas has worked; they have intrigued him so much over several years of observing them that he is preparing a new book on the "contemporary city." However, in the same way that *Delirious New York* was not in any way directly used as a project guide, this book, not yet a full manifesto but sufficiently sketched out to reveal its major lines of thought, will not necessarily be a direct reflection of preoccupations actually manifested in recent OMA projects,

Studies for a parking garage and TGV station
and for the Museum of Architecture and
Urbanism in Lille, 1988–1989

though it will not be totally removed from them.

Between *Metropolis*, or the city of vertical congestion, and *Flatland*, the city of two-dimensional figures imagined in science fiction—in which another form of congestion, horizontal this time, manifests itself, no longer regulated by the elevator but by the highway—new urban configurations appear; Rem Koolhaas's work involves exploring unforeseen perspectives. This work is all the more necessary because the crisis of urban planning or of *urban design*—disciplines even now incapable, both in their French and Anglo-Saxon contexts, of proposing a global approach to urban structure—has rendered the professionals who are supposed to maintain high standards for the discourse on the coherence between city form and city function impotent. Since the work of Kevin Lynch and Robert Venturi, precious few architectural analyses have addressed the visual questions raised by the superhighway or the commercial strip.[13]

The suburban world, which can simultaneously oppose the old centers and rural space, and which can be defined as the space of discontinuity,[14] is not really characterized by the absence of urban rules—which are only illusory—but rather by a saturation of rules, by the coexistence of multiple, usually incompatible systems. Long used for activities evacuated from the center, or waiting for access to the center, the peripheries today are welcoming new centralities, like those revealing the polarities surrounding Washington, Los Angeles, or Houston. Even in Paris, in an area surrounding Roissy airport, a new gate to the city has opened, a germ for a city of business and industry. The combination of high-

way interchanges, airports, and especially, innate reserves is at the heart of these operations where the individuality of architectural solutions is the rule, since the commercial programs are now entering into a competition as fierce as that which built the first skyscrapers at the dawn of the twentieth century.[15]

Rem Koolhaas could have chosen to "sublime this disorder" in his analyses and projects for the periphery.[16] He prefers to throw himself into research seeking unexpected manifestations of order, and especially seeking imagination and excellence in commercial buildings where these qualities are rarely betrayed. In his examination of Manhattan, Koolhaas has exhumed the figures of Raymond Hood and especially of Wallace Harrison. In pursuit of the "contemporary city," he discovered characters like John Portman and other virtuosi of development and hybrid architectures.[17]

From Atlanta to Seoul or Tokyo, but also in the Parisian periphery, Koolhaas brings to light a neglected professional culture, relegated to second place since, for better or worse, architecture became intellectualized. He enters into this enterprise with great curiosity for construction, for the most commercial written programs and for the symbolic force of the most "vulgar" buildings.

In counterpoint to an editorial project not yet completed, the pressure of the profession led him to take into account (undoubtedly earlier than he would have liked) the problems of the inner suburbs, notably with the winning competition entry for the new implanted center of the city of Lille, next to the TGV North station. The urban entity elaborated by OMA marks an important step for the team, but also, in its volume

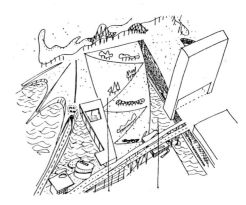

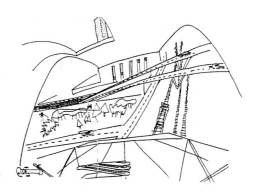

and its complexity, for the French architectural scene. The project reinterprets the urban fragments carved out by the railroad tracks situated between old Lille, today's center, the administrative center, and the *quartier* Saint-Maurice—where the ancient lines of the walls remained intact. Several formally differentiated polarities were expressed in the project: a raised urban park over a circular base; an urban services center running along the station in a great triangular block; a business sector occupying a block of highrise apartments, picking up the grid defining the plots and rows of an apartment complex across the highway; and finally, a service pole whose freer forms envelop and cross the tracks. The architectural solutions adopted for Lille undoubtedly call on a repertoire of forms closer to that used in the postwar reconstruction of Rotterdam than that used for the Atlanta suburbs. But the spaces of the "invisible metropolis" emerge as well: Koolhaas precisely develops the theme of superposition of networks and activities, taking so seriously the lines of the highways and their feeder roads that they become the primary material of the project. With ramps traversed by cars, trains, and subways, an efficacious scene of movement is proposed, diffracted in distinct programmatic and architectural sequences, as if OMA had wanted to mimic a process of negotiation and a collective project, or at least had anticipated it.

But notwithstanding the undeniably raw straightforwardness of the project, a sense of ambiguity, stemming certainly from its varied components, grew out of the whole, folding back on itself in a spider-web space, a kind of double inverse of La Villette. The idea of a "Piranesian space" in the lower levels of the project where these conflicts find their representation is no more, in fact, than a slightly gratuitous supplement to a project which is entirely sufficient in and of itself.

Understanding as a strategy

OMA's urban projects do not solely operate as responses to functional expectations, considered only in and of themselves with scant rigor, but rather as instruments of understanding. They are grounded in a particular reading of the city which, by itself, permits an appreciation of all the modalities. This strategy of reciprocal legitimizing between the project and the history takes as a unique twentieth century precedent Le Corbusier, whose manifestos of the twenties and thirties, based on observation of Paris's quandary or New York's "fairy-tale catastrophe," are closely associated with urban projects. The term "contemporary city" used to encompass Rem Koolhaas's ongoing research seems innocent enough, but serves only to underline this striking parallel. And if one looks from a different angle at the work of OMA as crystallizer of a professional strategy for responding to complex urban situations in the midst of the organizing paradigms of large European cities, Koolhaas's professional profile appears closer to that of Le Corbusier than to those of the architects of the 1970s and 1980s. If only people remembered the conceptual projects of Oswald-Matthias Ungers before the era of his gigantic quadrille construction sites or the territorial projects of Vittorio Gregotti . . . The sort of observation of the "contemporary city" Koolhaas practices is not transformed into a celebration of urban chaos tending toward an architecture which is a visualization or interpretation of that chaos. Koolhaas's inclusion in that ephemeral and improbable cohort of "deconstructivists" loses credibility when one examines his work, and moreover, when one is aware of his understanding and his noninstrumental interest in the constructivists, an attitude not shared by any of the other architects wrapping themselves in MoMA's label.

In contrast with the labyrinthine urban—and intellectual—chaos which the inventors of so-called "deconstructivism" believe they have discovered, one must read a manifestation of rationality in the work of the OMA. A rationality which seeks not only to render visible the conflicts between form and function, but which proposes as well to transfigure them by situating them in new logical networks. A rationality which is not that of the "*néant*," as Rem Koolhaas likes to say, but that of the interval.

Beyond the celebration of the New York metropolis and the discovery of the post-industrial cities, beyond the rehabilitation of Wallace Harrison and the interest in the anonymous architects of industrial parks, it is also necessary to see in Koolhaas another dimension. We know that the French version of the King Vidor film *The Fountainhead*, so dear to Rem Koolhaas, takes as its title *Le Rebelle*. He chooses to further the rebellion against the vulgar perception of large cities and the return to the fantastic dimension, as well as the rebellion against the uniformity of museum-like center cities resulting from an imitation of ancient ones, and against projects imitating urban chaos in their self-contained games with lines. For the countercurrent, for the great paradoxes, and with a call to the "eyes which do not see" the fragmented spaces of the modern metropolis (so important to the city), Rem Koolhaas proposes a strategy for the architectural reconquest of the cities. This strategy can doubtless be described and dissected analytically both in terms of land use and of the projects themselves, although OMA's visual brio is enough to feed the cohorts of epigones indifferent to the rational content of the method. But the rebellion is not simply a game with lines; more than a technique, it is a moral imperative.

1. Sigfried Giedion was one of the first critics to emphasize the "scientific" dimension and "laboratory" character of modern architecture. See Sigfried Giedion, *Bauen in Frankreich* (Berlin: Leipzig, Klinckhardt & Biermann, 1928).
2. See Rem Koolhaas and Gerrit Oorthuys, "Ivan Leonidov's Dom Narkomtjazprom, Moscow," in *Oppositions* 2 (January 1974): 95–103.
3. The promised monograph finally appeared in a translation from Russian: Selim O. Khan Magomedov, *Ivan Leonidov* (New York: Rizzoli, 1981) (IAUS 8), with an introduction by Vieri Quilici and a preface by Kenneth Frampton. On the subject of Leonidov, see the remarkable collection of documents prepared by Andrei Gozak: Andrei Gozak and Andrei Leonidov, *Ivan Leonidov, The Complete Works* (London: Academy Editions, 1988).
4. Rem Koolhaas, interview with Bruno Fortier, in *L'Architecture d'aujourd'hui* 262 (April 1989): 90.
5. See Wolf Tegethoff, *Mies van der Rohe—Die Villen und Landhausprojekte* (Krefeld/Essen: Verlag Richard Bacht GmbH, 1981).
6. See Rem Koolhaas, interview with Jacques Lucan, Patrice Noviant, and Bruno Vayssière, in *Architecture Mouvement Continuité* 6 (second series) (December 1984): 19.
7. Rem Koolhaas, interview with Patrice Goulet, in *L'Architecture d'aujourd'hui* 238 (April 1985): 7.
8. See Stanislaus von Moos, "Dutch Group Portrait Notes on OMA's City Hall Project for The Hague," in *A + U* 217 (October 1988): 87–94.
9. See Martin Steinmann, ed., *CIAM Dokumente 1928–1939* (Basel and Stuttgart: Birkhäuser, 1979).
10. See Bernard Huet, "La città come spazio abitabile, alternative alla Carta di Atene," in *Lotus* 41 (1984): 6–17.
11. See Bernard Leupen, *IJ-plein, Amsterdam, Een speurtocht naar nieuwe compositorische middelen* (Rotterdam: Uitgeverij 010 Publishers, 1989).
12. Regarding Ginzburg's projects, see, for lack of a more recent monograph, Selim O. Khan Magomedov, *Moisej Ginzburg* (Moscow, 1972; Milan: Franco Angeli, 1975 [Italian edition]).
13. See Donald Appleyard, Kevin Lynch, and John R. Myer, *The View from the Road* (Cambridge, MA: MIT Press, 1964); and Robert Venturi, Denise Scott Brown, and Steven Izenour, *Learning from Las Vegas* (Cambridge: MIT Press, 1972).
14. See Jean-Louis Cohen, "Per una architettura della discontinuità," in *Casabella* (Milan) 487–488 (January–February 1983); J. L. Cohen, "La discontinuité continue," in *Section a* (Montreal) III, no. 1; and J. L. Cohen, "Periferie e cultura della discontinuità," in L. Bazzanella and C. Giammarco, eds., *Progettare le periferie* (Turin: Celid, 1986).
15. See, regarding this competition: Thomas A. P. Van Leeuwen, *The Skyward Trend of Thought: Five Essays on the Metaphysics of the American Skyscraper* (The Hague: AHA Books, 1986).
16. This attitude is claimed by Alain Sarfati: see Alain Sarfati, "Projet pour la RN 7," in *L'Architecture d'aujourd'hui* 262 (April 1989): 86.
17. See Rem Koolhaas, "Atlanta, la métropole invisible," conference proceedings of 21 March 1988 (Paris: Centre Georges Pompidou, 1988).

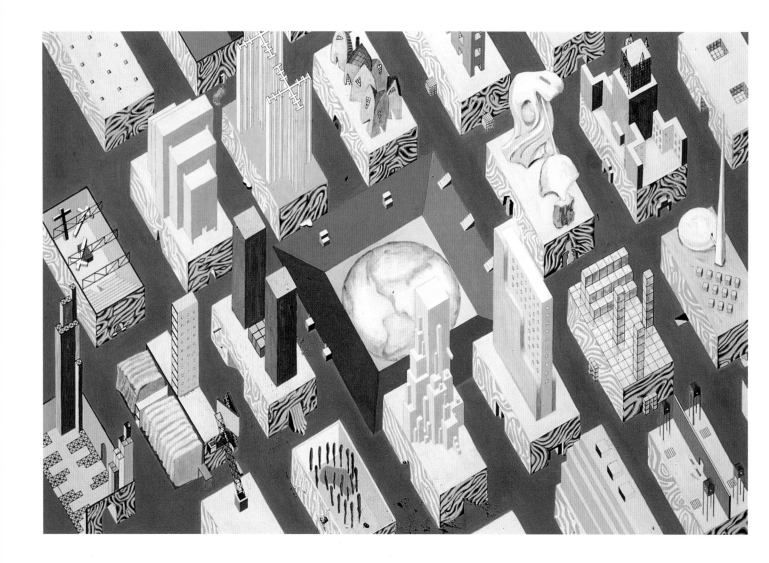

The Manhattan Transfer
Hubert Damisch

America and the question of modernity

What position does America occupy today, what role can it play henceforth in what is called the "formation" of an architect, if not in his or her culture? Of course, the question no longer carries the significance that it did at the end of the nineteenth century, when the young Adolf Loos, abandoning for a time his native Vienna, went to America, nor—by contrast—the relief experienced by Le Corbusier on his belated visit to New York in 1935. It remains important to the degree that, by a recurrence of circumstances, this same "new world" the image of which has played, by projection and in a fantastic or hallucinatory manner, a significant role in the crystallization and development of the idea of modernity (America, "scene of the life of the future"), this same world (this same America) is at present the scene of a radical questioning of the ideology called modernism, of which Europe can at best echo and which has found its privileged expression in the field of architectural criticism. There are numerous reasons for this, most prominent among which is the emigration at the end of the Second World War of many representatives of the Modern movement to New York, among them several Bauhaus masters who had already established a definitive pedagogical system. The consequence was the diffusion, within the American milieu and in response to its specific needs, of a singularly reductive and dogmatic version of the modernist program, a trivialized version of purely functional emphasis and one henceforth cut off from any activity qualifying as "avant-garde." A matter, one could say, of *translation* parallel to that carried out simultaneously by the avatars of psychoanalysis

under the effects of an analogous displacement or transfer.

Within architecture itself, it is symptomatic that the reaction in the United States that called for the banalization of modernist ideology borrowed the ways and terminology of the history of styles—whereas the apostles of the Modern movement claimed to have banished the very notion of style. This apparently calculated regression is proof of the desire to have done with that which constituted the most consistent program of "modernity:" to reduce architecture to a question of style, denying it any reality other than the strictly representative or picturesque, whereas the modernist project, as formulated during its brightest moment, recognized in architecture both the instrument of its realization and the proof (or the sign) of its fulfillment. The world, society, the entire edifice of human institutions was taken as something *to be constructed*, and this construction was to find monumental form, whether it be that the revolution seemed to constitute the necessary preliminary to the "housing problem" (architecture *and* revolution) or whether one saw in architecture a means of economizing (architecture *or* revolution), when one did not intend, as did the Russian constructivists, to put it to use. Jefferson's America took this project on its own terms: those of an essentially agrarian society feeling nothing but antipathy for the idea of the "metropolis" in all senses of the word—whether it was a question of colonial tutelage from which it had managed to free itself via a process that it would itself characterize as revolutionary or of the great urban agglomerations of which a Europe in the process of rapid industrialization was beginning to present the horrifying spectacle.

When the United States was itself stricken with the sickness, the divorce was soon consummated between those subscribing to an anti-urban ideology and those—promoters, engineers, architects—who, in Chicago and New York, saw themselves as artisans of a new culture. On one side were the adepts of the prairie school, led by Frank Lloyd Wright, for whom the solution to demographic sprawl lay in turning the entire country into one gigantic *suburb*; on the other, the builders of skyscrapers, of what Le Corbusier called "Titanic mineralogy, [dressed] in a violent silhouette like a drawing done in a fevered state"[1] on the edges of the Loop or the rock of Manhattan. The problem—insofar as the opposition could remain tenable under this form of caricature—was thus to know on which side "modernity" was situated: the attitude of compromise adopted by the European emigres shows that the real question lay elsewhere, resting less on form or style than on the terms in which modernity could be set in motion, here and there.

To return to the question with which we began (What role can America play today in the formation and culture of architects?), it is clear that this concerns not only European architects (to say nothing of Japanese, Chinese, Latin Americans, etc.).

I have cited several reasons why the debate (or so-called debate) on modernity was born in America and particularly in the field of architecture. But if it is true that such a debate had relevance in the American context, if it is true that it had or should have had, in this context, some relationship, paradoxically, to modernity in a more universal sense and that it might aid in better articulating the issue and in indicating the stakes, the identification of America as the chosen land is indispensable to all men of art, on whichever edge of the Atlantic or Pacific they reside, beginning with those who are still novices or apprentices. And that goes for American architects as well. To be (or want to be) American is not necessarily a given, and least of all for artists and architects, who participate for better or worse in a history in which America has no assigned point of entry. Prepared as it was by, among other things, the work carried out at the Museum of Modern Art in New York by men such as Alfred Barr and the same Philip Johnson who now presents his work under the rubric of "postmodernism," the transporting to the United States of a considerable number of European architects and artists at the end of the thirties and the correlate translation of the modernist ideology into the vernacular language was not enough to alter fundamentally American architects' and artists' awareness of their own situation, their own *position*. That would have required that the distance (distance from Europe, but also distance from the American context) that made a singularity of their situation or position itself turn inside-out, with the exotic becoming the indigenous or familiar, itself always threatened by the possibility of becoming its opposite—unsettling, unfamiliar, uncanny. The reaction against the trivialized and banal version of modernist ideology prevailing in the United States assumed a "European" connotation all the more paradoxical, at first sight, because the ideology was itself a product of importation. But in order that the grafting could occur with ease and with such effects, it would be led by certain critical minds who expected the profession to interrogate itself concerning the eminently complex and even contradictory relationships that America was able to maintain (and continues to do so, albeit too late) with "modernity"—regardless of how one interprets the term, which is of course exactly part of the question.

The flying Dutchman

Consider for a moment an apprentice from the Old World whose debut consisted of linking the practice of the architectural profession to an almost schizophrenic, but in fact deliberate and controlled, mode of geographic vagabondage: story, and I mean *story*, because this is not simply a theoretical matter, of permanently exposing his professional life to the same force of transfer that displaced the issue of modernity, historically speaking, from Europe to America, with the above-mentioned effects. This same apprentice soon departed from Holland, and after four years at the Architectural Association in London, following 1968, headed for the United States, with the idea of a work about New York already in mind. But *work*, what does that mean—and why on New York? If the point of departure (Holland) is at all significant, it is not only because the first settlers of Manhattan were Dutchmen who made sure to recreate on this savage land a bit of their home country, going so far as to carve a canal framed by gabled houses out of the rock. Holland, moreover, is not merely a land of nostalgia: from Berlage to Oud and Bakema, from Van Doesburg to Mondrian, Holland provided an ever-active contingent in the battle for "modernity," often of programmatic aspect, even though often meeting with political and institutional resistance.

Rem Koolhaas must have experienced this the hard way upon returning to his native land. But can one even speak of a *return*, since he set no limit on the constant aerial peregrination that led him to return regularly to America—as if driven incessantly to repeat the movement that first took him there? If Koolhaas learned anything from his transatlantic voyages and his work on New York, it was that the conditions of a practice claiming to be avant-garde—if the concept still had any meaning—as much as the eventual forms of his exercise had changed radically since the era of the "historic" avant-gardes, to the degree that it is difficult today to conceive of the possibility of such a practice and to recognize its necessity, and that one is led to see, in the attempts to link up again with "avant-garde" language and practices, only a form of comedy in which nostalgia contends with a strictly repetitive, almost unconscious rhetoric. The reconciliation was certainly not designed to trouble Koolhaas, but he did not relinquish the idea of avant-garde activity, at least in architecture; moreover, if he claimed the title for his own work, it was because he knew how to formulate the clearest idea of what the stakes, as well as the field of applications and the points of impact, might be. That is to say, rare thing today, that Koolhaas is in possession of both a project and a theory, of a strategy and an ethic—the problem being to understand that this project and theory, this strategy and ethic, cannot be separated from the force of displacement or the effects of transfer mentioned above, and, what is more, that it is there that they find their condition and upon which they depend. If there is to be an avant-garde work today, it

will not *take place* in the sense that the historical avant-gardes occurred in predetermined contexts. It will be of everywhere and nowhere (which is not to endow it with a "global" dimension) and will by necessity pass through a distancing (and suspense) of which the airplane flight is a metaphor. The fact is that the "historical" avant-gardes themselves could not have been constituted, instituted, or recognized as such except at the cost of a displacement and, in one way or another, a transfer. The first futurist manifesto was published in Paris in the *Figaro*; Theo Van Doesburg's activity as a traveling businessman is well-known; and the encounter in Berlin of a Soviet artist like El Lissitzky and a German architect like Mies van der Rohe is emblematic of the birth of an international, if not internationalist, avant-garde. In the same way, one hears that America, as provincial as she was on the artistic map, would never have heard about the avant-garde if not by procuration and through intermediaries, themselves displaced, such as Gertrude Stein and Ezra Pound, from which arose the nostalgia expressed by certain American architects today who, more or less consciously and more or less cynically, are putting back in circulation, adapted to the tastes of today's American public, formulas derived from the avant-garde of the twenties. The analysis would not be admissable if America had known the avant-garde directly. Koolhaas's accomplishment is to have demonstrated, with his extraordinary talent as a historian (as much as Walter Benjamin's pioneering first work "Paris, Capital of the 19th Century," *Delirious New York* is a great work of history), that between 1890 and 1940, Manhattan was the site of a work qualifying as avant-garde but occurring through routes entirely different from those of the European avant-gardes, beginning with the fact that this work involved neither a self-conscious, organized avant-garde nor the publication of any manifesto. And better (or worse) yet, it could only develop and produce its effects because it proceeded from an unformulated, if not unconscious, theory.

The strategy of Manhattanism

It is this theory that Koolhaas sought to bring to light in *Delirious New York*, as he added a new term to the catalogue of "isms" supposedly corresponding to various movements and that establishes the rhythm of the history of modern art. As opposed to the numerous manifestos that remained dead letters, the program of "Manhattanism" was unique in that it could only come into creation by renouncing all explicit enunciation, by actors refusing to adopt a discourse that ran contrary to the reality of their practice. The divorce or radical dissociation between acknowledged intentions and effective plans not only marked the most constant line of development in Manhattan, it also constituted, according to Koolhaas, the key to the *strategy of its realization*.[2]
What has gone unnoticed is that this strategy, this program, this theory, by remaining implicit—the growth of New York, like that of Chicago, takes on the appearance of a natural process if not cataclysm—went directly against what would become a dogma of the modern movement. "It is a catastrophe," said Le Corbusier on arriving in New York, while adding, "but a beautiful and dignified catastrophe."[3] As if the "ecstasy before architecture" (Koolhaas's phrase) that—taste, ideology, and style aside—no one in

New York (or Chicago) can escape, as if the fascination of the "stupefying city" was irresistibly impressed on the apostle of the Ville Radieuse, while still retaining his dogma, which dictated that there could be no new architecture without a new urbanism. *Radieuse* ("radiant"), New York was not, at least in Le Corbusier's sense of the term, since it did not meet the terms of which he had become the world's propagandist. But beautiful, assuredly, and wonderful, even though this savage beauty and wonder looked to him like an invitation to begin again, to set everything in motion in order, in his terms, to move "toward something even greater, but controlled."
When Le Corbusier discovered America, it was to reconnect with the discourse of the original settlers and adopt their principles, the same principles that Koolhaas—citing an 1849 work on New York—called *exterminators* and that led to the systematic elimination of "savagery" (another name for "barbarity") and its replacement by more refined, more "civilized" forms of life. But barbarity and civilization are interchangeable terms: one is always a barbarian to another, if not to oneself. The same Le Corbusier quickly characterized New York as a "savage city" yet admired its diamond glitter. "What disorder, my God, what fury! What perfection already, what promise! What unity on the molecular level: checkerboard streets, office upon office, compact crystal. Sublime and atrocious, yet nothing works. All that's left is to see clearly, to think, to conceive, and to begin again." In conclusion, a characteristically peremptory first-person passage: just as there is no way to eliminate savagery except to exterminate the savages, leaving a clean slate which one

can occupy and upon which one can take things into one's own hands: "Yes, I was going about it the wrong way. Let us begin again!"[4]
The Americans didn't wait for Le Corbusier to begin all over again. On the "theater of progress" that is Manhattan (but if it is indeed a theater, how would one describe the scenery?), "the spectacle can neither end nor advance in the conventional sense of dramatic progression; it can only cyclically reproduce a single theme: the irrevocable entanglement of creation and destruction, perpetually replayed."[5] The exterminating principle continues to operate: "What is at one moment refinement becomes in the next moment barbarity." Yet these principles could only operate in the strictly defined, regulated, and controlled framework that was the continuous development of Manhattan according to the grid imposed by the 1811 plan, when the majority of the island was still uninhabited, and that conferred on the orthogonal grill of the colonial tradition an unusual, almost phantasmagoric scale, the growth of the metropolis assuming from this moment onward the appearance of an experiment in limits indefinitely renewed.
One couldn't find a better illustration than the genealogy of the New York skyscraper as traced by Koolhaas, a structure born of the encounter, within the well-defined matrix, of three distinct urbanistic innovations: the proliferation made possible by the new technology of stacked stories each repeating the groundfloor plan while multiplying it, with its eventual form impossible to foresee in advance; the tower, itself a symbol of technical progress as well as of a lofty autonomy of a necessarily defiant air; and finally

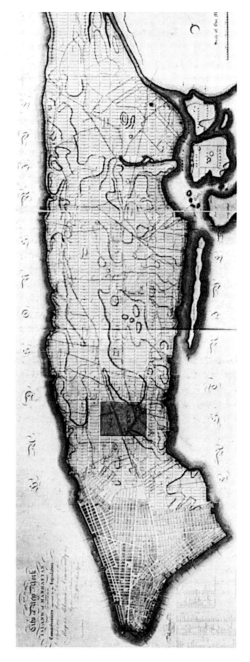

the "block" defined by the intersection of four rectilinear arteries meeting at right angles and that represented the a priori limitations, within this framework, of all architectural and urbanistic enterprise. A limit on the ground level, according to the philosophy of the grid, and its two-dimensional configuration in plan, but also a limit in volume if not height, since it called for a corrective: the process of territorial reproduction (the multiplication pure and simple of the parceling plan) could only result in chaos, under the influence of a form of natural selection in which the gauge of individual success was measured by the destruction of the surrounding area. The 1916 zoning law introduced a stricture that Koolhaas justifiably calls "architectural murder" determining for each island or block of Manhattan "an imaginary envelope that defined the contours of the maximum allowable construction."[6] As limited as it was in application to the dimensions of the block, the law nonetheless traced the contours of Manhattan's final form, defined as a *mega-village* consisting (as the grid insisted) of 13 x 156 = 2,028 "houses." It was left to a "perspectivist" like Hugh Ferriss to envision the end results of the piecemeal process dictated by the 1811 plan by rendering in charcoal phantomlike masses, rigorously stripped of all superfluous detail as well as of any stigma of eclecticism, destined to become—to recall the title of the book Ferriss published in 1929, the year of the crash—those of the *Metropolis of Tomorrow*.[7] The 1916 law was intended to limit protrusions that the imposition of the grid could not contain, despite the avowed intentions of the authors of the 1811 plan: protrusions that, while contained by the block system,

assumed an air of natural catastrophes. The legend that architects in New York as in Chicago were instruments of a growth of which they were not in control and the implications of which they poorly measured seems confirmed by the fact that when the moment came to question themselves concerning the new forms of urbanism, they could only improve upon the fatality of a development pushing the city even higher into the sky: the skyscraper is "inevitable," and all that one can do is adapt, building ever higher, to free up space on the ground and to insure the maximum circulation of air and light—and automobiles. The image proposed by Harvey Wiley Corbett of a *Modernized Venice*, in which automobile traffic would be separated from pedestrian traffic, which would be displaced to arcaded sidewalks one level above the street and connected by a web of bridges and footbridges, an image that assumed utopian dimensions via the metaphoric transfer on which it was based, well reflects the ambiguity of the discourse of the skyscraper theoreticians: "The theory, insofar as it exists, will adapt to the skyscraper and not the skyscraper to the theory. . . . In order to obtain for the skyscraper permanent authority to cause congestion, they threw themselves, apparently, into a crusade in favor of decongestion."[8]

The skyscraper and the montage of attractions

Le Corbusier concurred: "The skyscrapers are too small!" (even though he judged them greater than their architects). But his own program was unequivocal. What he kept of the American skyscraper was first of all that it introduced new dimensions—in expanse and height—to architecture, as well as the new equipment that made such

Volumetric study based on
the zoning codes of 1916,
drawing by Hugh Ferriss

structures possible. To begin with was the elevator that carried one, without mishap, to the sixty-fifth floor in the time it took, in Paris, to walk to the sixth, with the corollary that indicates the difference in scale between the two types of urban dynamic: in Europe, the introduction of elevators into apartment buildings in affluent neighborhoods permitted the privileged to move to upper stories up to that time relegated to servants; in Manhattan, the invention first presented to the public in the context of the 1853 fair made possible the infinite multiplication and diversification of the urban scene, at each level and in forms of which the Old World could have no idea. And it was this that the allegedly unconscious adepts of Manhattanism were unwilling to renounce (but to call them "unconscious" is completely different than to see them only as agents in the service of Capital, in both its speculative and bureaucratic forms). Le Corbusier could well affirm that the formidable force of human destiny characterizing the skyscraper should decongest the ground by spacing out taller buildings.[9] He saw in the skyscraper, however "Cartesian" it might be, a tool destined to fulfill specific, essentially bureaucratic functions: "In Algiers, one skyscraper will do; in Barcelona, two; in Anvers, three. . . . The cities of commerce will be vertical, with enormous green spaces." The skyscraper scene in Manhattan, however, was completely different (but this Le Corbusier neither could nor would have wanted to see, any more than the skyscraper theorists would have known how to or wanted to *say*). The Manhattan of Manhattanism was a city of commerce but also a meeting place and pleasure spot which the skyscraper emulated, the Metrop-

olis offering to its inhabitants the spectacle inscribed in stone, concrete, and steel of a style of living according to a completely different program, responding to needs completely different from that of mere "lodging." From one scene to another (from one modernity to another, but it was all one), the point of view changed radically: in the Ville Radieuse, everyone was to enjoy at home sun, light, and a view extending to the horizon; from the tops of the skyscrapers (as from the top of the Eiffel Tower), the metropolis multiplied for the sake of one who was there only as a spectator (as when, in Paris or New York, one stood on or crossed a bridge),[10] plunging views of the city and promises of all sorts of pleasures that the city contained in its depths and at each of its levels, ad infinitum. Nothing better illustrates the difference between these two versions of modernity, one that objects to the very idea of the "metropolis" and one that carries it to the point of excess, than the effect of the bird's-eye views made possible by tall buildings as by airplanes (and, today, helicopters). A spokesman of modernist ideology such as Walter Gropius, founder of the Bauhaus who emigrated to the United States in 1936, counted among the advantages of the terraced flat roof the fact that cities viewed from airplanes would disappear, leaving no sign of the buildings buried under greenery.[11] As for greenery, Manhattan would content itself with the considerable but strictly defined 153 blocks of Central Park, framed today by residential apartment buildings and skyscrapers of which the oldest terminate in pyramids or needles piercing the sky. But the creation of this park in the middle of the nineteenth century did not conform to the desire to inscribe the city of the future in a natural framework, as the ideology of the Ville Radieuse stipulated, except in the determination to reserve in the middle of the island a model of nature that would permit the measurement of the evolution of the site in the context of the metropolis yet to come: "a taxidermic conservation of nature illustrating for eternity the drama of nature overtaken by culture,"[12] in imitation of the great national parks first conceived at that time, which also signified the conquest of the West and the myth of the "frontier"—a myth in which the skyscraper participated in its own way, up to the limit set on its vertical thrust. With this exception, that Olmstead's Central Park was the product of a series of manipulations visible in a way that they were not at Yellowstone or Yosemite: "a tapestry of synthetic Arcadia," as Koolhaas described it, of which the diminished equivalent, at the end of the twentieth century, would be a garden of several square meters near Houston Street displaying specimens of the flora existing on Manhattan Island before the arrival of the Europeans. Apparently the creators of Central Park perceived what was to become characteristic of the metropolitan condition: the obliteration of nature and the triumph of artifice carried to the point of phantasm under the combined effect of density and of a culture that exploited all new technical resources to play deliberately the game of *congestion*. Yet these things could not become the object of any explicit enunciation. Let us repeat: the program of Manhattanism could not have succeeded in imposing and inscribing itself on reality except by remaining unformulated, when theoreticians did not speak the language, taken for "modern-

ist," of decongestion in order to give the skyscraper a chance. Raymond Hood, the architect who best incarnated the spirit of modernism, long kept secret his vision of the future Manhattan as a city of independent, rival towers before publishing—in the year of the Wall Street crash—his *City Under One Roof*, which proposed that the only solution to the congestion engendered by skyscrapers was the creation of enormous, interdependent ensembles and the regrouping of entire branches of industry, clubs, hotels, boutiques, apartments, and even theaters, which would minimize the number of horizontal surface displacements on the ground level by substituting vertical displacements within buildings.

Rockefeller Center—of which Hood would be one of the principal designers—offered "the most articulate demonstration of the implicit theory of Manhattanism, which proposed the simultaneous existence of several programs on a single site linked only by the common elements of elevators, service conduits, columns, and the external envelope."[13] This theory found, as early as 1931, its first illustration in the Downtown Athletic Club, the thirty-eight floors of which offered to metropolitan bachelors a complete gamut of sports equipment, artificial scenery, meeting rooms, and bedrooms, between which shuttled elevators: this "machine to engender and intensify the most desirable modes of human relationships" responded on all levels, in a different political and cultural context, to the idea of the skyscraper as "social condenser" introduced by Alexander Pasternak (the brother of Boris) in 1926, while offering at each level and in each stratum a fragment of the "montage of attractions" (in Eisenstein's sense) that was the reward of metropolitan existence but that eluded planning. One often hears that America has no monuments: the skyscraper instigated a new category, the "automonument," that reflected only itself but that could not avoid, because of its volume, becoming an empty symbol open to all signification and to all manner of "history."[14]

Memory games

Displacement, condensation: it is no accident that these two words correspond to two operations characteristic of unconscious processes and of dreams above all. Koolhaas's work on New York presents in effect all the traits of an anamnesis in the analytic sense, and how could it be otherwise, since the task he set himself was to translate into words the unformulated, if not unconscious, program of which the Manhattan *skyline* is the visible manifestation? The architect has a right to the unconscious—the formula works for the analyst as for the analysand, while it is not always possible to determine which is the plaything of the other: the architect, manipulated as he is, in his innermost being by forces springing from the culture's unconscious, or the unconscious itself, upon which the analyst elaborates in the slightly mad hope of beating it at its own game.

And the game is linked with those of memory. If it is true that in psychic life nothing is lost and all is conserved in one way or another, to return if need be, can we not compare it, asks Freud, to what the archaeologist reveals to us of the history of a city—beginning with the so-called "eternal city," to which he returns throughout his work? As Freud observes, if everything from the successive stages of Rome was conserved, one

would arrive at absurd representations since, for example, it is impossible to translate in space the way in which monuments could have stood on the same place in succession, other than depicting them side by side. The comparison doesn't entirely work, yet Freud was apparently unwilling to renounce it, if only (to believe him) because it shows "how far we are from grasping in visual terms the characteristics of the life of the mind."[15] But why was it necessary to call on the visible or figurative, if not because the mind itself, from moment to moment, endures it?

According to Freud, the archaeological metaphor fails in that the hypothesis of an integral conservation of the past can not be applied to the life of the mind unless the psychic medium remains intact, whereas the development of a city supposes deliberate destructions. Because the terms of the comparison can be reversed, and the psychic metaphor played with to clarify, in the manner of the images borrowed from the life of the mind, certain turns and detours of the urban and, even more, metropolitan memory. We know that catastrophes can provide occasions to reconstruct on different sites buildings that have, historically, made room for others (as was done during the reconstruction of Varsovie). But this is what matters, *a fortiori*, for the "capital of perpetual crisis" that is Manhattan, Manhattan of which the development is the very image of the functioning—displacement, condensation—of the unconscious. One thing at least is preserved intact throughout the history of the metropolis: the grid, never questioned or altered (the only twists allowed consist of rounding or perforating the angles of blocks, as do far too many of today's

architects) and that has functioned since the beginning as a memory device of unequalled rigor.

This device dictated that any operation that could be characterized as "urbanist" assume an architectural form and by necessity inscribe itself within the limits of a single block (Hood's *Manhattan 1950*, which proposed the erection of thirty-eight "mountains" at the intersection of the grid's principal arteries if anything underlined this constraint). This rule had its consequences, some quite real and material, others of the imaginary or fantastic order, when not ascribed to the symbolic developments, tied as they were to each other, to the effects of condensation as well as displacement authorized by the block system. Koolhaas has shown how the montages of attractions of all types that made Coney Island a success served to incubate the mythology and thematic of Manhattanism, while a veritable "technology of phantasm" found its testing ground there. But it was necessary, in order for this technology to bear fruit, to transfer it to Manhattan and set it within the grid. The consequence of such a transfer was not the substitution of reality for phantasm. Rather, it was the phantasm that, to achieve the form and coherence of architecture, took the shape of reality. When, on returning to New York after spending thirty years in Europe, the protagonist of Henry James's "The Jolly Corner" tries to take account of the novelties, differences, and "bignesses," the "enormous grandeur" that greets him everywhere he turns, it is because he is troubled about the "phantoms" that will undoubtedly disturb the conversion of the house in which he was born into a skyscraper. Undoubtedly, the operation allows him to show his sentimental side. But the fact is that the transformations of Manhattan seem to have obeyed, from the beginning, the rule of psychic life ensuring that nothing is lost at any stage of development; the past can always return in one form or another when the occasion arises. Here again what one is tempted to take for a natural phenomenon exhibits all the aspects of a calculated strategy. When, under the orders of William Waldorf Astor, the family residence originally constructed on the site of a farm was itself replaced by a hotel, the architects were instructed to preserve as much as possible the aura of the house: "For Astor, the demolition of a structure in no way impeded the preservation of its spirit; with the Waldorf, the concept of reincarnation was introduced into architecture. . . . The recovery, be it literal or merely on the level of nomenclature, of elements from the Astor residence suggests that the Waldorf-Astoria was conceived by its promoters as a house haunted by the ghosts of its predecessors. To build a house haunted by its own past and that of other buildings, such is the strategy employed by Manhattanism to produce a substitute history."[16] But the time would come when, the value of the block having increased, it would become necessary to destroy the hotel to make way for a skyscraper that would surpass all others as much by its size as by its beauty: whereas the idea of the Waldorf (a "residential unit" adapted to the exigencies of modern life) would reappear, displaced, at another point on the grid, the Empire State Building, which assumed certain elements of the previous structure (beginning with the elevator cages) raised the specter of architectural cannibalism in

which the final edifice incorporates the power of the previous occupants of the site and perpetuates their memory. "The Empire State Building is . . . the apotheosis of unconscious Manhattan. The Waldorf is the first realization of conscious Manhattan,"[17] but both were only made possible by miming, to the point of giving them the appearance of history in good and due form, the procedures of the unconscious.

A novel of apprenticeship

Written as it was by a young architect just beginning his career, *Delirious New York* presents all the aspects of a *bildungsroman*, of a "novel of apprenticeship" or of "formation": just as often happens in the genre, the experience related is that of a conversion of which it is the means rather than the end. The young Koolhaas knew perfectly well what he was looking for in New York and what the consequences of such a transfer, and the work of anamnesis that it made possible, would be—the novel of the formation of the architect mixing with that of the metropolis itself. Manhattan, capital of a twentieth century, was now coming to a close, in the same way that Walter Benjamin saw Paris as the capital of the nineteenth century? If Koolhaas intended to draft the *retroactive* manifesto of Manhattan—and of Manhattanism—it was not just as a historian with retrospective but with critical and even polemical goals: it was for him a matter of guarding against oblivion where the debate on modernity threatened to carry in its wake the culture of the twentieth century that had lost none of its actuality: "Like urbanism, Manhattanism is the only ideology nourished from the start on the splendor and misery of the metropolitan condition—

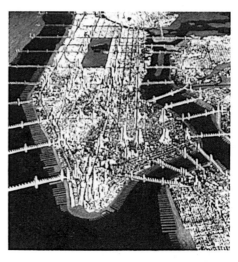

hyperdensity—without ever ceasing to believe in it as the sole foundation of modern culture. . . . The retroactive formation of the Manhattan program is a polemical operation. It exhibits certain strategies, certain innovations, and certain theorems that not only confer logic and order on the past existence of the city but from which the current validity argues for a renewal of Manhattanism, this time as an explicit doctrine capable of transcending its insular origins to claim its place among contemporary urbanisms."[18] This book which proposes, via the image of Manhattan, "a plan for a *culture of congestion,*" is thus the fruit of a proper analytical work. Work of memory as much as of explicitness (the two aspects being inseparable) and that intended to (re)establish the architect in the position of subject in a history of which he had been dispossessed by a repression, of which one essential object was the culture of modernity.

To see in film the art form par excellence of the twentieth century (the only *living* art, with architecture, as Panofsky declared, barely founded in New York in 1933) was not necessarily to imply that one had lost sight of painting or theater any more than "new images" impose themselves on the field already considered "post-film." The problem was to take the measure in each case of the repression that constituted one of the means of this incessant forward thrust, and of the loss that resulted in terms of historical experience. Thus it continues for this *other* culture of modernity (or this culture of an *other* modernity) of which Manhattan was the laboratory at the same time that it created the scene and the lesson of which one prefers to ignore today in order to retain only its decorative aspect. If Koolhaas continues obstinately to denounce the fatality that makes each generation reject the heritage of the preceding one, if he claims for his part that of the last great architects of Manhattan (up to and including Wallace K. Harrison, who gave form to the Le Corbusier's purely theoretical proposition for the United Nations headquarters), it is for reasons other than nostalgia, reasons that assume, in the present context, a precise strategic sense: at a time when the discourse on architecture has been reduced to questions of style, while the criteria for judgment prevailing in matters of institutional choices are essentially descriptive and promotional, it is symptomatic that it was left to an architect to defend before and against everyone the eminently "modern" notion of *program,* opposing to the cult of the sign and of simulacra the reality of partially unconscious processes that confer on the project of a "metropolitan culture" the weight and force of desire.

1. Le Corbusier, *Quand les cathédrales étaient blanches* (Paris: Plon, 1937): 52.
2. See Rem Koolhaas, *Delirious New York* (New York: Oxford University Press, 1978): 69.
3. Le Corbusier, 101.
4. Ibid., 90.
5. Koolhaas, 10.
6. Ibid., 90.
7. Hugh Ferris, *The Metropolis of Tomorrow* (1929; reprint, New York: Princeton Architectural Press, 1986).
8. Koolhaas, 100.
9. "The skyscraper should not be a coquettish tuft of feathers on the pavement. It is a prodigious instrument of concentration to be planted amid vast open spaces. The density of the skyscraper and open expanses at its base necessarily function together. To have one without the other, which is what has happened in New York, is a catastrophe!" Le Corbusier, 82.
10. It was while waiting on the Pont Neuf to go get her glasses from the optician that Maxime Du Camp conceived the idea of writing about Paris, the book that the Classical historians have not written about Athens, Rome, or Carthage, a project which Walter Benjamin would take up (see Walter Benjamin, "The Paris of the Second Empire as seen through the eyes of Charles Baudelaire," in *Charles Baudelaire: A Lyrical Poet at the Apogee of Capitalism*).
11. See Walter Gropius, *The New Architecture and the Bauhaus* (London, 1935): 30.
12. Koolhaas, 17.
13. Ibid., 164–170.
14. See ibid., 81.
15. Sigmund Freud, *Civilization and its Discontents.*
16. Koolhaas, 111–112.
17. Ibid., 114.
18. Ibid., 7.

Flagrant délit, from *Delirious New York*
OMA-Madelon Vriesendorp

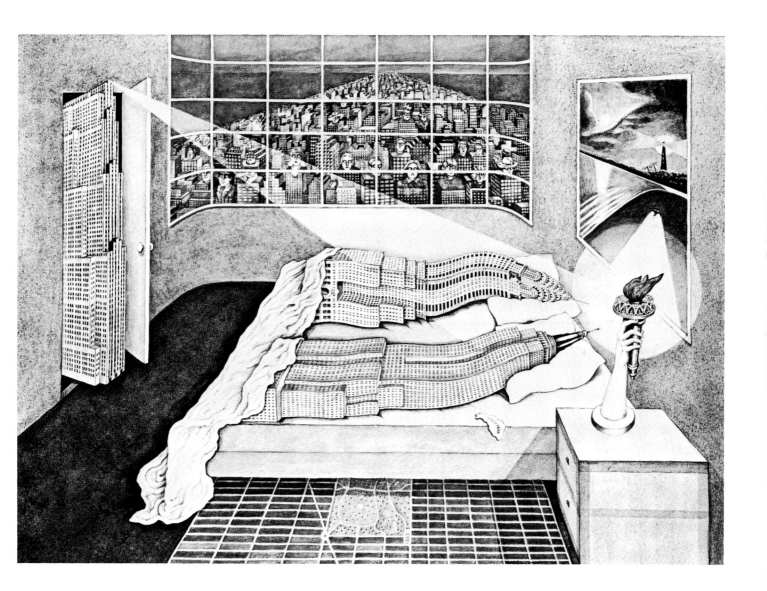

Study for the Boompjes apartment
building and observation tower,
Rotterdam, 1980–1982

The Architect of Modern Life

Jacques Lucan

I'm horrified by the fatality that leads each generation to contradict the preceding one.[1]
Rem Koolhaas

Rem Koolhaas's remark permits us to understand many of the stances and characteristics of OMA's architectural and planning projects. Not to be led astray by a fatality, in this case not to align with a morality of *ressentiment* that dictates a dogmatic rejection of all that the preceding generation thought and produced: such an attitude explains how Rem Koolhaas often appears to shift with regard to his colleagues for whom radical criticism (and the ensuing rejection) of theoretical and constructed architectural and urban projects after the Second World War—and, by way of teleological consequence, the rejection of the premises of the 1920s and 30s—is an indispensible prerequisite to all new affirmation. During the 1970s and early 1980s, a consensus of uncertain contours was effectively reached on the question of urban architecture and the reconstruction of the (European) city. This consensus rested on the belief that it was once again possible to give a coherence and a homogeneity to recent and ongoing urban developments, to find again the sense of "city." This movement was fed with nostalgia, and often remained blind to unclassifiable phenomena, foreign to the usual categories, that architects for the most part refused to apprehend, too fearful that the phenomena would thus be recognized as disasters that they lacked the intellectual means to understand, let alone control. Rem Koolhaas forbade himself to close his eyes, as Robert Venturi had several years earlier when he "discovered" Las Vegas . . . he forbade himself all hysteria of vision exclusive to historic centers; he stigmatized the "eyes that do not see" the *metropolitan dimension* of contemporary urban phenomena.

Theory of retroaction

To open one's eyes to contemporary realities necessitates a double movement. The first movement: do not leave to oblivion those bits of history in which today's emblematic realities of our "modern condition" were formed. From this point of view, in particular with *Delirious New York*, Rem Koolhaas is not so much an historian as an *archaeologist* when he brings to light the logic of development, sometimes with the help of documents not chosen or gathered in by traditional histories. Not to leave to oblivion those bits of history is necessarily not to narrow one's interests, to expand one's horizon, to allow more opportunities for understanding and, perhaps, for new parameters of intervention.

Rem Koolhaas thus affirms: "We have often verified the law that states that the richest ideas are left in the dustbin of history: the more discredited on the plateau of good taste, the more innovative on the plateau of content."[2]

The second movement: to be constantly on the lookout for manifestations of that which we will call, in the words of Charles Baudelaire, "*la vie moderne.*"[3] Calling on Baudelaire here is not mere pedantry: Rem Koolhaas often cites the poet who loved to contemplate "the eternal beauty and the astonishing harmony of life in the capitals," "the landscapes of the great cities,"[4] to discover and extract the "mysterious beauty,"[5] the "fantastic reality of life,"[6] the character of that which he himself called "modernity:" "All the visible universe is but a store of images and signs to which the imagination assigns a place and a relative value; it is a patch of pasture the imagination must digest and transform."[7]

Rem Koolhaas, when he studies the contemporary metropolis, and in particular the world of the peripheries, does not content himself to consider them as dictionaries of errors to be redressed; he holds up their "terrifying beauty"[8] and disdains the method of "*systematic* idealization," the "automatic overestimation of the extant."[9] Not satisfied with this extant, he seeks to exploit all of its potentialities.

Rotterdam was in this regard exemplary, since after the reconstruction of the 1950s, which remains a paradigm of "modern" planning, it was subjected to anti-modernist revisions that tried to forget the quality of its voids and its open spaces to further a compact densification. The celebrated "Slab Tower, Tower Bridge" project, situated on the banks of the Meuse, is an attempt to reforge a broken chain while securing the most difficult, narrow terrain for the construction of a vertical edifice next to the quais: tangible sign of a desire not to forget that which forms Rotterdam while proposing a new synthesis of contradictory conditions.

The double movement I have previously described, that of an archaeologist and that of a "painter of modern life," demands a *retroactive logic*. This logic immediately tries to establish when all architectural and planning projects began to base themselves on "the most clinical inventory of the actual conditions of each site, no matter how mediocre"[10]—that which Baudelaire called the "store of images and signs to which the imagination assigns a place and a relative value." This logic is carried moreover by an indefatigable optimism: "Even in the most degraded situations, one can always find the beginning or the key to something good.

[. . .] There are no situations sufficiently rotten where we cannot reach a retroactive concept"[11]—which Baudelaire may have explained like this: "The spectacle of elegant life that circulates in the bowels of a big city [. . .] proves to us that we have only to open our eyes to know our heroism."[12]

To open our eyes: that has now become a necessity for understanding the essential characteristics of certain of OMA's projects. Also in Rotterdam, for example, the project for an office building at Churchill-plein, one of the principal intersections of the city, situated at the boundary of the center city and the harbor zone, surrounded by historic ancient and modern buildings, is a proposal for a "contextual" skyscraper which, while respecting a defined exterior, turns one of its inclined facades toward the center of the city, the other toward the port. The building stands on the site not so much as a structure "which imposes on it," but as a reflection of the conditions of the environment. Another example, this time in The Hague, is the National Dance Theater, which inscribes itself in a site in transition populated by heterogenous buildings. OMA did not seek with this theater to reorder a chaotic ensemble with the affirmation of a forced monumental order: that would have been a chimera. They accepted that which Rem Koolhaas himself called an "*cadavre exquis*" to be fabricated with parts of a program already defined at the time of a previous project that was to be constructed on another site (at Scheveningen), under the constraints of a general context whose lines of transformation OMA did not control, and even with an insurmountable next-door neighbor: a concert hall constructed by another architect. From this telescoping of intensely

exploited conditions resulted a kaleidoscopic edifice, which some people considered incoherent, but which nonetheless conserved an exceptional programmatic coherence. Retroactive logic, this action of returning to the environment, accords a legitimacy to an architectural project, while at the same time it inscribes itself in a rational dimension: to persuade clients, OMA often uses a series of images or schema; they permit us to appreciate the development, the stages of reasoning, with a demonstration; they seem to succeed each other in an ineluctible fashion towards a result that, "as fate would have it," could be nothing else but that which is presented to us. Certainly we must known that things are not so simple and the work of OMA is full of hesitations as well, of deliberate choices, which are not the simple consequences of "scientific" deductions, but remnants of this *rational will*, that Koolhaas sometimes wants to be "suffocating," marking all of OMA's projects and placing them outside all nostalgia: retroactive logic has nothing to do with regret or some notion of *revival*, with a return to the past, a retrogression; it resembles more than anything a "Hegelian" optimism.

An architecture of relative neutrality

To take seriously any context, whatever it may be; to suppose that it always has something to reveal to us about our condition and to give to us; that in return we must ameliorate it and transform it: this philosophy takes control in an attitude with a reciprocal relationship to the architecture itself, an attitude that Rem Koolhaas summarizes when he recalls the objective he followed with the National Dance Theater of The Hague: "We wanted it as innocent as possi-

Office building at Churchill-plein,
Rotterdam, 1984, volumetric
studies and view of the model

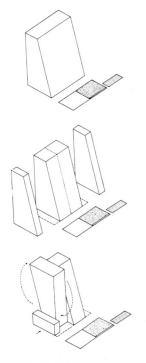

ble, deciding to integrate ourselves in a contemporary project, without trying for a minute to critique it, to convert it, to smile at it."[13]

This selective and controlled restraint is indispensible if one does not wish the new project to be an affirmation of arrogance that has the excessive pretense to convert, to force compliance with one's order on an already heterogenous ensemble. It is also knowing how to take measure of urban situations that can only be "reformed" with subtle means, by injecting them with a dose of instability. For Rem Koolhaas, too many projects effectively bit the dust for not knowing how to evaluate their impact on an environment which was, for them, only circumstantial. We understand why he sometimes revolts against "the obstinacy of architects," their "repugnance for empty space,"[14] their "terrible desire to make architecture,"[15] and that he seeks a "relative neutrality": "For me, the most attractive proposition is essentially to build in a non-pretentious, intelligent manner [. . .], a relatively elegant manner, but also to build relatively neutral things."[16]

Relative neutrality is neither a swoon, a disappearance, nor a timid modesty; it is more immediately a synonym for a *simplicity* which only reveals its restrained complexities to attentive examination, which only divulges its density of intention and its mystery so long as one makes the effort not to be satisfied with an impatient, immediate, instantaneous vision. From this point of view, the National Dance Theater at The Hague is exemplary, as are the two rows of housing on the IJ-plein, resulting from precise typological work which, with renewed

research, will be pioneers of modern architecture.

Relative neutrality is also a synonym for *abstraction*. Architecture will pay no heed (or very little) to an emphatic, expressionistic dimension that constantly offers up traces of intervention from the hand of the architect, traces of his ideology.

This explains why Rem Koolhaas exhorts us to "accept modern architecture without neurosis,"[17] and why he is in particular interested in the products of the 1950s shaped under *tabula rasa* conditions by architects who were "involuntary prisoners"[18] of architecture, a production where, he goes on to say, "the unconscious of modernity could revel in a sort of pure state which has and still does fascinate me."[19]

This position justifies an apprehension of problems relative to construction outside any "naturalist" response: the use of materials does not give rise to an expressionistic construction, to an insistance on modes of assemblage and articulation—often pretexts for demonstrations of virtuosity.

The equivalence between architecture and construction sometimes calls for sophisticated solutions; here they conserve a discretion which insinuates ambiguity and foreignness. Thus, at the National Dance Theater, a cable surreptitiously, obliquely, crosses a window that opens on the rehearsal studios; in the concert hall, subdued light glitters on the metal lines of the suspended ceiling, to be defined by the contours whose generating principle is practically dissimulated. At IJ-plein, on the roof of the longest of two rows of housing, the two slightly shifted circular arcs are not decorative motives, even if they have the undeniable power to evoke the rays of the rising sun; they are instead

IJ-plein, Amsterdam, 1980–1989,
structure of the building with
view of the passageway
to the street

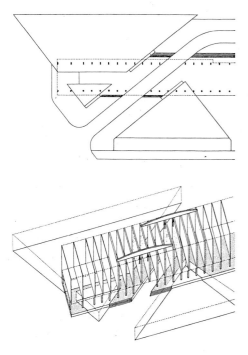

girders necessary to support the internal walls which establish a regular repetition of partitions. These girders were essential here because the pilotis could not have provided the necessary support: a road needed to pass underneath.

OMA's architectural realizations thus do not insistently seek to bring onto the scene the prowesses of technological order. On the contrary, we witness a space of sober, but voluntary, sublimation of ordinary materials, "richness" coming often parsimoniously underlined by restrained parts of buildings. A "high tech" dimension is not requisite here to form the image of architecture and its "modernity": we will see that this "high tech" dimension is more often expressed in the exploitation of programmatic conditions, in the very content.

A recurring history

The desire to remain relatively neutral, itself tied to the adoption of a retroactive logic, is not found solely in reports on contextual architecture or at the construction site. It is not singularly the consequence of a pragmatic, realistic attitude, more lucid regarding the conditions surrounding contemporary situations. It is attempting as well to fix the rules of conduct concerning the doctrinal affirmations of today . . . and of yesterday.

Rem Koolhaas, in the manner of several architects, guards against peremptory declarations—and this undoubtedly explains his constant reticence with regard to Le Corbusier and his "theories." He prefers to focus his attention on projects effectively designed or constructed to extract or retain their value as recommendations for the present. At IJ-plein, the urban study started with a comparison of several seminal projects of modern architecture located in the perimeter of the area, a comparison that allowed an evaluation of the differences between the opposing occupancy alternatives. In Berlin, with its proposition for Kochstraße and Friedrichstraße, OMA centered its intervention not on the ignorance of preceding projects but on the rediscovery of those by Mies van der Rohe, Mendelsohn, and Hilberseimer; the intention was to re-establish the historical continuity of a horizon of comprehension and conception, and to counteract as well the natural penchant of doctrinaire architects: "An architectural doctrine is adopted to be inevitably replaced, a few years later, by the opposite doctrine: a negative sequence in which each generation can do nothing but ridicule the preceding one. The effect of this succession of yes-no-yes is anti-historical, because it reduces architectural discourse to an incomprehensible string of disjointed phrases."[20]

In place of these disjointed phrases, the last of which, paradoxically, would be uttered by the "city reconstructors," does OMA seek a new continuity for architectural and urban discourse?

The answer to this question can only be ambivalent. Because the cult of negativity in the succession of doctrines and in their built consequences results in an individualism that characterizes modern artistic production, the hope of a consensus, a synthesis or a newfound continuity is fundamentally illusory; it could only be satisfied by a veritable regression. Just the same, OMA seeks to register continuities when existing relationships between buildings and programs are weak, fragile, or inconsistent. Thus, for

Bijlmermeer's "*grand ensemble*," which, starting from 1976, Rem Koolhaas argued should be left unfinished, describing it as a Las Vegas of the social democratic state, OMA defined two crossed bands that house the most important programs and functions, a sort of *cardo* and *decumanus*, orthagonal coordinate axes that accentuate the sliced-up territory while giving it a principal orientation. The Bijlmermeer project can equally well appear to be a criticism of the inherited planning principles of CIAM and Team X as a faithful elucidation and extension of the same principles achieved after several years of uncertainty. It must finally be noted that the Bijlmermeer project, following the example of several other OMA planning projects, projects the optimistic, "heroic" conviction that planning enterprises are always valuable: planning is not a discipline to be tossed into the dustbin of history, particularly when it addresses itself to the recently colonized territories that are our suburbanized peripheries, which define the city less often as *cité* and more as limitless agglomeration, as metropolis. In this light, Elia Zenghelis, longtime collaborator of Rem Koolhaas and cofounder of OMA, affirms: "Architecture, for us, only holds any interest, only is possible when it lends a certain intelligence to an inanimate ensemble."[22]

Thus we understand the power of New York and its grid to fascinate: it is the zeroth degree of a territorial partition sufficient to establish community, the continuity of independent parts, to "join the sentences." Even if "each block is [. . .] *isolated* like an island, left to itself,"[23] even if Manhattan is transformed into an "archipelago of blocks"[24] and if the resulting system is a "system of solitudes."[25]

The *cardo* and *decumanus* of Bijlmermeer can also appear to be a substitute for an absent grid. For the competition for La Villette, for projects destined for the 1989 Universal Exposition, then for Melun-Sénart, all of OMA's work dealing with *bands* will be an attempt to establish a base on which architectural events can take place: events foreseeable and unforeseeable, individually controllable or uncontrollable, results of programming avatars and successive abandonment by developers. The architect will be placed in a situation in which he often cannot grasp anything palpable; his vision will no longer fix on frozen traces, compact, monumental, and built; he will more often work with the void; he must "*imaginer le néant*"[26]: "More important than the conception of cities is—and will be more and more in the immediate future—the conception of their decomposition."[27] The planning proposed by OMA is thus not so much an "urbanism of good intentions,"[28] as of rapidly contradictory intentions, fueled by the succession of doctrines and the reversals of tendencies. It is not, however, devoid of "civilizing" objectives and never abandons the hope of rendering intelligible, thus intelligent, the supposed disorder of the contemporary city. It attempts to integrate the conditions of change, as if the project did not anticipate reality but rather was perpetually in pursuit of it, in the search for the greatest proximity.

It doesn't astonish us that the image of the architect held with particular fondness by Rem Koolhaas is that of a surfer on a wave: the force and the direction of the wave are uncontrollable, it breaks, the surfer can only, in exploiting it, "master" it by choosing his route . . . .

Programmatic instability

The succession of planning doctrines, their divergences and oppositions, does not need to be apprehended only in a negative way. They participate as well in the phenomenon of instability that characterizes "modern life" and which one finds, often in the most flagrant manner, when one pays attention to the broad programs proposed to today's architects. These programs effectively integrate a multitude of diverse, complex, and contradictory demands. Sometimes at the start of a competition, these demands are not even defined with precision; either the project attempts to reveal the exact tenor of the demands, to singularize, to bring to them individual solutions and to articulate the ensemble of solutions, or the project offers a global response that easily permits modification, alteration, or programmatic substitution without loss of overall cohesion.

With the competition entry for the new City Hall for The Hague, it is without a doubt the latter solution OMA adopts. This solution explicitly opposes an attitude which Rem Koolhaas characterises as "European,"[29] where "the elements state: 'I am a library,' 'I am the offices,' 'I am the entrance,' where there is such an intense competition between the different components that the overall effect is stupid or ridiculous in appearance."[30] To explain OMA's project, Rem Koolhaas made reference to the "lesson"[31] he learned in New York: "Starting at a certain scale, it is important that a building has its own integrity, its own limpidity, its own sculptural or architectural

quality, and in the interior of its envelope the different programs can develop almost like caves or like autonomous projects, a building whose envelope plays its role in the life of the city and responds to all the demands of its context."[32] The project's general envelope for the new City Hall in The Hague takes the form of an enormous complex, composed essentially of offices, situated on the border between the old center and the immediate periphery; it results from a parallelism of three different bands across different faces. The decomposition of the built mass multiplies the visual tableaux and the depths; it makes possible on this site the presence of a vertical ensemble at the same time that it permits the relatively free distribution of a program still marked by indeterminacy.

One understands now Rem Koolhaas's assertion: "I combine architectural specificity and programmatic instability,"[33] and that the seriousness with which the question of program is addressed is indispensible: it is taking into account the conditions of the program that invest the project with its premier rationality, ahead of any recourse to figures or to traditional hierarchical processes for the distribution of elements.

One takes part in a sort of immersion in a functional density, from which arises not so much an expression of existing functions, but first a *form* capable of integrating components marked by instability.

It is there that all of OMA's projects, from the Parc de la Villette to the Center for Art and Media Technology at Karlsruhe, take up again and project the problem of functionalism. They also rediscover certain traits of some architectural projects by members of Team X, which attempted in their time

to get out of the rut of an architectural fixation on creating a form for every function. Was it not the team of Candilis-Josic-Woods that, for the competition for the Free University in Berlin in 1963, claimed they substituted the notion of organization for that of composition to define a structure that associated a diversity of changing activities?

In this light, Rem Koolhaas is implicitly opposed to that which one could call the "Dutch tradition," which has often sought to define architectural specificity separate from all instability. Who was not astonished by the obsession contained in the celebrated Schröder house, where each space, each portion of space, each piece of furniture was without a specific use, even knowing that "flexibility" was the objective sought in partitioning the rooms? This determination, this excessive "humanization" of architecture, surfaces again with the two most well-known contemporary Dutch architects: Aldo van Eyck and Herman Hertzberger. If Rem Koolhaas admires their programmatic will, he also expresses his reticence regarding "a sort of imprisonment in the very precision and humanity of the architectural interventions."[34] The fascination for certain of Mies van der Rohe's projects is explained *a contrario* through their abstract dimension and that assures that houses with patios, for example, are "always complex enough to be interpreted as grids, to be like labyrinths."[35] Grids and labyrinths: is this not the opposition between a principle of stability and a depth of instability which one finds in the project for the Parc de la Villette and in the 1989 Universal Exposition, in the project for the National Library of France as well as in that for Karlsruhe?

Theory of congestion

Up to this point I have not called upon the important principal thesis contained in *Delirious New York*: "a plan for a *culture of congestion*,"[36] "an argument in favor of a renewal of Manhattanism" as "explicit doctrine, capable of claiming its place among the contemporary urbanisms,"[37] knowing that "the architecture of Manhattan is the paradigm of the exploitation of density."[38] If I have voluntarily delayed in examining this thesis and its consequences, it is for two principal reasons.

The first reason: not to evaluate each of OMA's projects solely by the standards advanced in *Delirious New York*, as if everything in that book perhaps already had been stripped of some of its power: "When I wrote it [*Delirious New York*], I decided not to become obsessed with it, to forget it without trying, as people evidently were waiting for me to prove the correctness of the thesis, which I spend my time proving with my projects."[39]

The second reason: the definition of a "culture of congestion" is a sufficiently seductive thesis to obliterate those that accompany it, so as a result we would be more attentive to complex articulations, to declensions of a conception of architecture and planning.

Do these two reasons suggest that the thesis of a "culture of congestion" is, in the final accounting, not important to an understanding of OMA's projects? Certainly not. *Delirious New York* is not an exercise in and for itself, for the pleasure of erudition; it is a *manifesto* addressed to us and which effectively gives the basis for a conception and a larger intelligence to the work of those who follow it. The "culture of congestion" thesis now can illuminate for a brighter day the ideas

I've just developed here: the understanding that the universe of "modern life" always turns under the influence of congestion, knowing that "the culture of congestion *is* the culture of the twentieth century,"[40] and that the example was given to us in New York by the "theoreticians of the skyscraper."

OMA waited for the proper moment to manifest its ideas with force. This occasion was offered in 1982–83 with the competition for the Parc de la Villette: the project to design a park for the twenty-first century was inaugural; it clearly marked a crucial step in the development of a body of work. On an area resembling a substratum of the city, in an almost "experimental" situation, OMA proposed not a "*design*" but a "strategy," "a "*method* combining at the same time architectural specificity and programmatic indeterminacy;"[41] they expressed a formal analogy between the plan with its parallel strips and the section through the floors at the Downtown Athletic Club;[42] they exploited all possibilities for confrontations and regulated superpositions to affirm a density of occupation almost without (built) architecture.

The same work was pursued, again in almost experimental terrain, with the projects for the Universal Exposition of 1989, having first aspired to intervene in the realm of an urban periphery with a large complex, at Bijlmermeer, then in the realm (for the moment "empty") of a new town, at Melun-Sénart. In these two last cases, OMA was confronted with metropolitan situations of another sort, which must necessarily accommodate heterogenous programs because of their breadth and even their appearance, often cast out of historic centers, where the void is the dimension that must be controlled before the advent of architecture, where historic models are of little help in defining the lines of an urban plan, where a new type of urbanity, which perhaps no longer has a name,[43] must be manifested and has already been manifested.

The project for the City Hall at The Hague represented a supplementary step where "congestion" is exploited not in a principally horizontal dimension, but in a vertical one. This project inaugurated a new series that was enriched in 1989 with the project for Zeebrugge, with that for the National Library of France and with that for Karlsruhe. These three projects were conceived at the same time, with a common aim, and thus they can be compared: they put in place the same principles, each time in a different manner, in consideration for the given programs. This did not result in identical architectural responses, but rather the exploitation of density and of congestion remains always the conducting wire to purpose. With the project for the National Library of France and that for Karlsruhe, we take part in the investment of the city with edifices more congested than the city itself: a single building is composed of numerous components and multiple connections. The National Library of France and the Center for Art and Media Technology at Karlsruhe are "tableaux" that tell us that urban density can only irrepressibly increase, but that this increase would be for the collective benefit: a mirror image of a world that must multiply its activities to the same rhythm as its means of communication and of knowledge.

Elia Zenghelis affirms: "Everything relating to nature, essentially, is doomed to disappearance. We are born, we die, we disappear; only ideas, art, the artificial seem to offer some promise of permanence."[44] Rem Koolhaas affirms: "The final function of architecture will be to create symbolic spaces responding to the persistent desire for collectivity."[45]

1. Rem Koolhaas, "La deuxième chance de l'architecture moderne . . .," interview with Patrice Goulet, in *L'Architecture d'aujourd'hui* 238 (April 1985): 7.
2. Ibid., 7.
3. See Charles Baudelaire, "Le Peintre de la vie moderne, 1863–1868," in *Œuvres complètes* Vol. II (Paris: Galimard, la Pléiade, 1976, all other citations of Baudelaire are taken from this same edition): 682–724.
4. Ibid., 692.
5. Ibid., 695.
6. Ibid., 697.
7. Baudelaire, "Salon de 1959," in *Œuvres complètes*, 627.
8. See Rem Koolhaas, "The Terrifying Beauty of the Twentieth Century," in *OMA/Rem Koolhaas*, 154–155.
9. Ibid., 154–155.
10. Ibid., 154–155.
11. Koolhaas, "La deuxième chance," 6.
12. Baudelaire, "Salon de 1846," in *Œuvres complètes*, 495.
13. Koolhaas, "La deuxième chance," 8.
14. See Rem Koolhaas, "Imagining the Nothingness," in *OMA/Rem Koolhaas*, 156–157.
15. Rem Koolhaas, "Entretien avec Jacques Lucan, Patrice Noviant, et Bruno Vayssière," in *AMC* 6 (December 1984): 20.
16. Rem Koolhaas, "I Combine Architectural Specificity with Programmatic Instability," interview with Jaime Yatsuka, in *Telescope* (Tokyo) 3 (1989): 7.
17. Koolhaas, "Entretien avec Jacques Lucan," 20.
18. Rem Koolhaas, "Trente ans après," interview with Patrice Goulet, in *Les Années 50* (Paris: Centre Georges Pompidou, 1988): 474.
19. Ibid., 474.
20. Rem Koolhaas, in *L'Architecture d'aujourd'hui* 238, (April 1985): 22, in the text accompanying the presentation of the project for Kochstraße-Friedrichstraße.
21. See Rem Koolhaas, *Amsterdam: An Architectural Lesson*, ed. Maarten Kloos (Amsterdam: Thoth Publishing House, 1988): 114.
22. Elia Zenghelis, ". . . Ou le début de la fin du réel," interview with Patrice Goulet, in *L'Architecture d'aujourd'hui* 238 (April 1985): 12.
23. Rem Koolhaas, *Delirious New York* (New York: Oxford University Press, 1978): 79.
24. Ibid., 79.
25. Ibid., 120.
26. Koolhaas, "Imagining the Nothingness," 156–157.
27. Ibid., 156–157.
28. Koolhaas, *Delirious New York*, 65 et passim.
29. Rem Koolhaas, conference at the University of Delft, 10 April 1987, in *Indesem 87—International Design Seminar* (Delft: Delftse Universitaire Pers, 1988): 214.
30. Ibid., 214.
31. Ibid., 212.
32. Ibid., 212.
33. Koolhaas, "I Combine Architectural," 7.
34. Koolhaas, "Entretien avec Jacques Lucan," 18.
35. Koolhaas, "I Combine Architectural," 11.
36. Koolhaas, *Delirious New York*, 7.
37. Ibid., 7.
38. Ibid., 7.
39. Koolhaas, "La deuxième chance," 4.
40. Koolhaas, *Delirious New York*, 104.
41. Rem Koolhaas, presentation text for the Parc de la Villette, in *OMA/Rem Koolhaas*, 86–95.
42. See Rem Koolhaas, "New York/La Villette," in *OMA/Rem Koolhaas*, 160–161.
43. See Koolhaas, *Amsterdam*, 113–114.
44. Elia Zenghelis, ". . . Ou le début," 14.
45. Rem Koolhaas, presentation text for the National Library of France, in *OMA/Rem Koolhaas*, 132–139.

The New Sobriety

Two Villas with Patios

Rotterdam 1984–1988

These two villas, parodying the section of the traditional Dutch house, were constructed on an embankment intended for a highway that never saw the light of day. To the north, the road is below ground level. The entrance is there, underneath the living space. To the south, the site borders on a canal.

On the main floor of the house, a patio, more or less square, is disposed in such a way that it generates, together with a free-standing wall, the living spaces of the house: a living room to the south, a dining room to the north.

The wall separates two "rooms": a bedroom and a study, which are connected by a secret passage that opens onto the bathroom.

The garden facade brings together four different kinds of glass (armored, clear, frosted, and green tinted) which create intensities, transparencies, and opacities. The metallic east wall of the patio belongs to the kitchen; the north and the south sides are sliding glass doors; the patio is surfaced with glass plates, giving light to the gymnasium below.

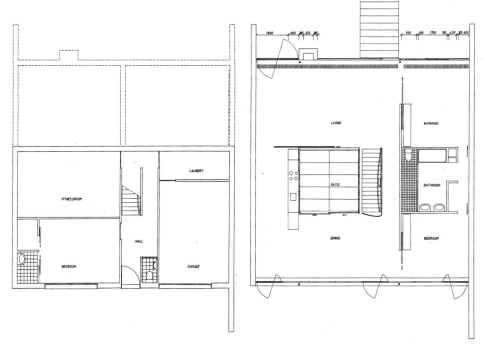

View of the street facade
and plans of the lower
and upper levels

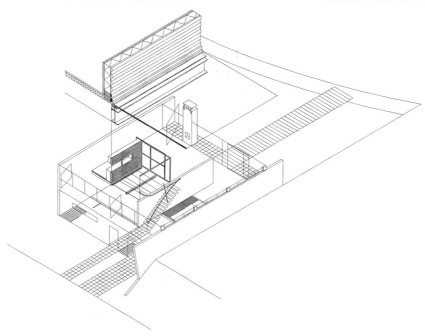

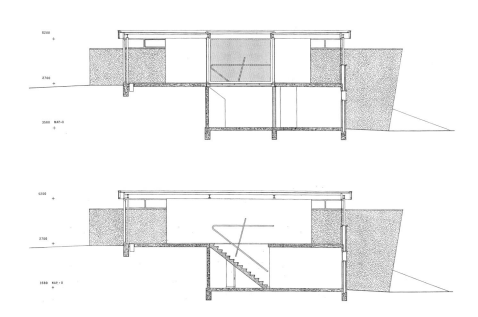

National Dance Theater

The Hague 1980–1987

The first and second projects for the National Dance Theater join offices, dance studios, ateliers, housing for the dancers, and a theater with a capacity of 800 seats, equipped for opera as well as dance. These projects were to be built in Scheveningen, the bathing resort nearest The Hague, seat of the royal court; they were to be situated on a site abutting an old dome-covered theater, recalling the tent which housed the summer festivals in the last century.

The first project was conceived as a rehearsal facility with an open-air theater which could be covered by a tent. In the second project the hall was covered by a metal roof, whose structure is based on a sophisticated use of materials common to industrial buildings. The roof's undulations evoke the image of a tent. The third built project is located in an entirely different context in the civic center of The Hague. The most important part of this city quarter is allocated for new governmental offices. The context is characterized by the presence of two towers, the (eventually to be completed) ramp of an abandoned urban highway, a major axis leading to the Parliament, the site of the future city hall, and a seventeenth-century church, sole witness to the historic city. On this site, designated for cultural use, the Dance Theater is coupled with a concert hall (Van Mourik, architect), and constructed over a parking lot shared with a hotel whose architect, Carel Weeber, has effectively defined the urban layout of this area. The fourth element on the site is a square in front of the old church.

The original design intention, a functional box decorated with flamboyant exterior elements in harmony with the vernacular resort architecture, became, in the institutional center of The Hague, a banal facade which revealed little of the interior.

The interior public spaces were conceived as voids hollowed out of the envelope. The hall now has a capacity of 1001 seats. The foyer is located in a seven-meter-wide space between the concert hall and theater itself, extended under the sloping floor of the latter. Also disposed in this space are a half-moon balcony and a floating oval satellite, the *Skybar*, suspended by cables.

The roof above the hall and the foyer is self-supporting, with steel beams placed according to the inverse of the generating curve. The second project's roof is thus maintained but, reinforced by an intermediate metal girder, takes on a more important dimension. Between the stage/hall area and the row of three floors housing ateliers, offices, and dancers' lodgings is located a group of three dance studios. A perpendicular row groups the services for the dancers: sauna, pool, massage rooms, and showers. A circular restaurant faces the public space.

The structure of the theater is essentially metal; on the interior, aluminum cladding is employed alongside plasterboard covered in stucco, marble, or gold foil. The use of color is emphasized on the interior, whereas the exterior is decorated with more muted shades—black, white, grey, metal.

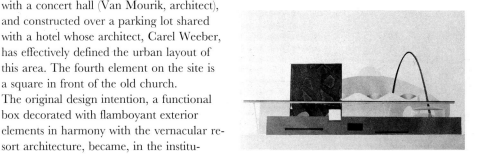

Exterior view of the theater, rendering of the second project for Scheveningen, and axonometric of the final version at The Hague

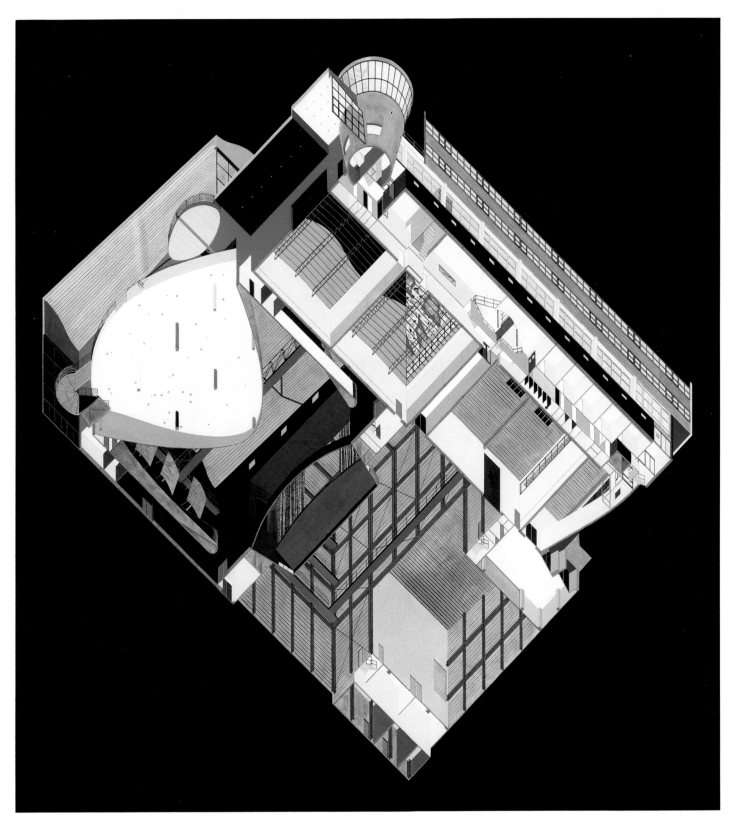

Exterior view with the two towers of the
Ministry of Justice in the background

SHIRASAGI

View of the rear facade

Longitudinal section through
the foyer and theater and
plan of the ground floor

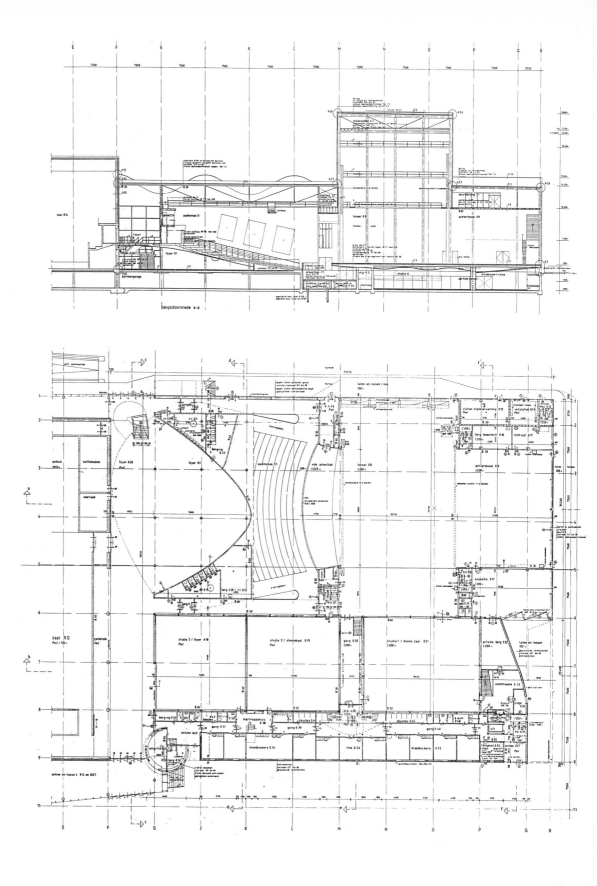

Transverse section through the foyer
and plan of the balcony level

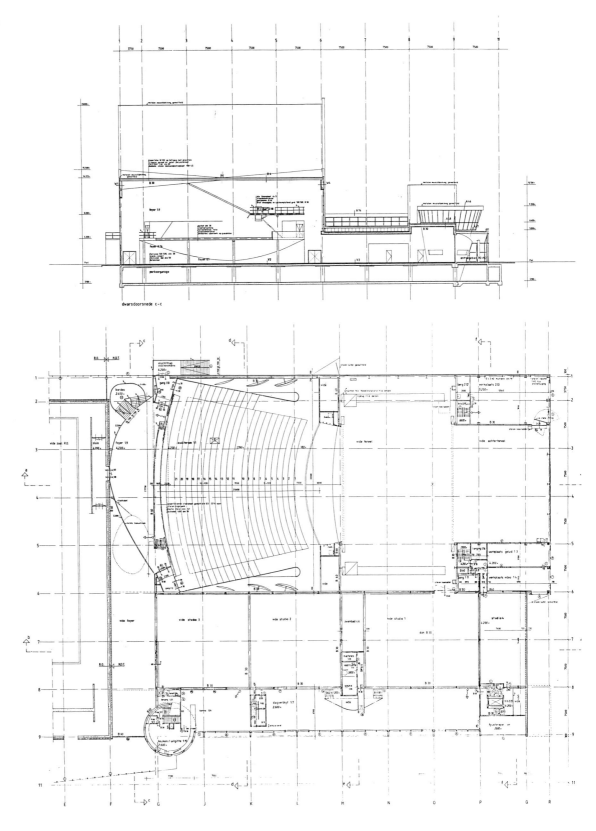

The balcony with the *Skybar* in the background

Access corridor to the theater and
view of the interior of the hall

City Hall
The Hague 1986

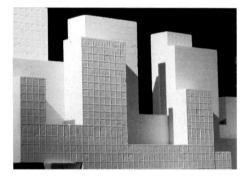

Located in the Forum district in the center of The Hague, this project houses facilities for municipal services, information offices, a public library, rentable office space, and other commercial uses.

Responding to the uncertainties of the program at the time the competition was announced, this project was designed to offer possibilities for adaptation, translating programmatic instability into architectural terms. The program demands a useable area ten times greater than the area of the site. From this requirement arises the massive quality of the building, which occupies an important place in the heart of the city. The site is a triangle whose shortest side is oriented toward the west. The north and west facades are aligned on the primary circulation axes. To the south, a pedestrian street links The Hague's central train station to a commercial center located to the west. The mass of the rectangular building, concentrated in the north, contrasts with an enclosed triangular piazza leading to the plaza in front of the performance halls (the concert hall and National Dance Theater) and to the raised plaza in front of the hotel.

The building is composed of three parallel slabs, linked by a six-storey mass. The middle slab houses an eight-storey void, creating a monumental hall. The mass of the building decreases from the seventh to the twenty-third floor. Each slab measures 14.4m x 240m. The figure of 14.4m is a multiple of 1.8m, the basic dimensional module for Dutch offices, and allows daylight to penetrate throughout.

Games of displacement and detachment among the three tall slabs create towers of different forms. Underneath are housed the information services, the offices, the municipal council hall, and the library. The municipal offices are distributed throughout the towers, while the commercial offices are grouped in an eastern tower.

From a technical point of view, the load-bearing walls allow an eventual rearrangement of the office floors, up to an office occupying the maximum area of each of the three rectangles.

The north facade, which looks out over the historic heart of the city, is clad in stone. The south facade consists of a stainless steel grille. The north and south "interior" facades are curtain walls. On the east and west facades concrete-paneled walls are pierced by small windows.

Both the public and employees enter City Hall from the west. Delivery and other services enter from the north; commercial tenants from the east. The library, café, and restaurant are oriented toward the south, and look out over the pedestrian street and square. The council hall, spherical in form, overhangs the entrance hall. The public accesses upper levels, particularly the library, by escalators that stretch along the south facade. On the third floor, a commercial gallery extends along the north facade and the entrance hall to the library, joining with the commercial offices to the east.

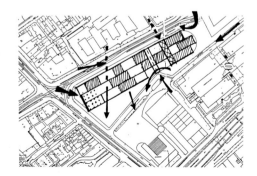

Model views and diagram of
the bands of different levels

The insertion of the project in its context,
the footprint of the site, and the area
occupied by the building

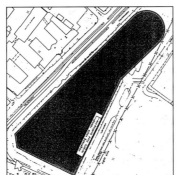 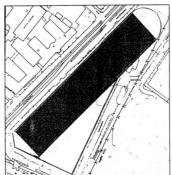

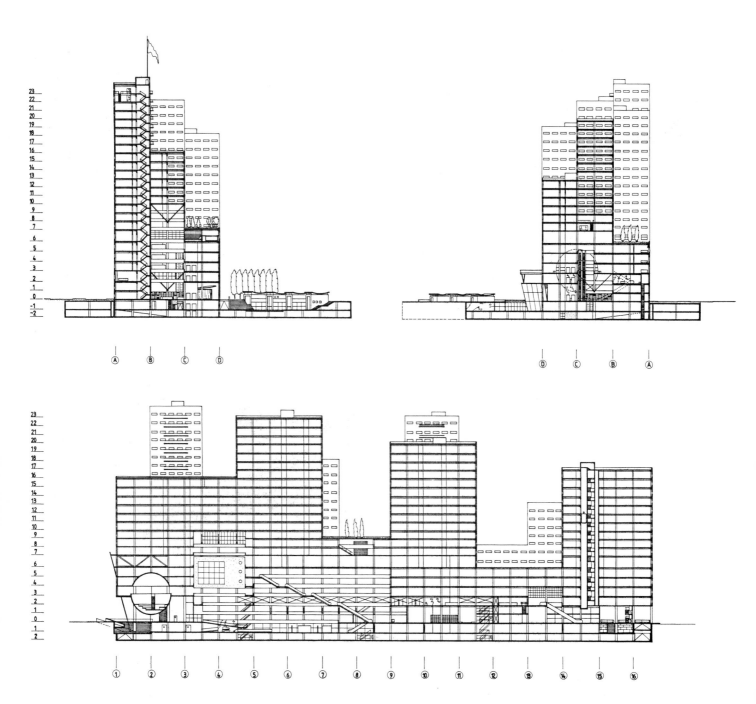

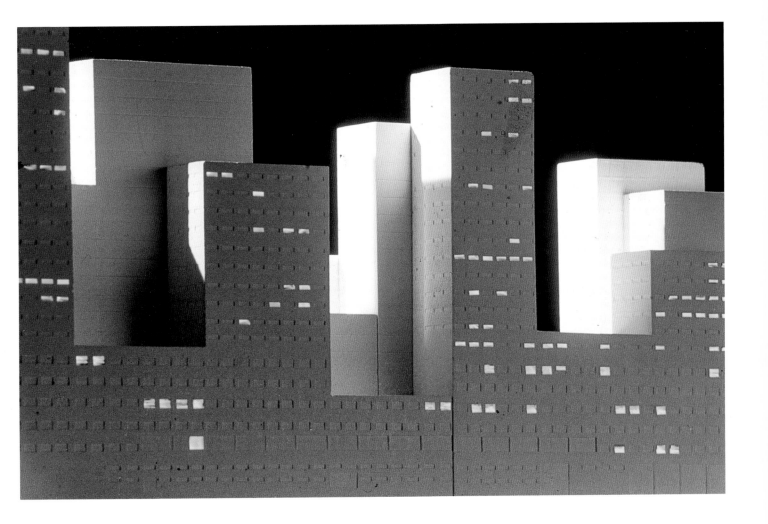

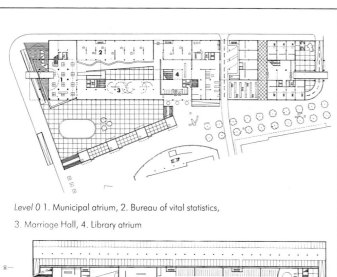

Level 0 1. Municipal atrium, 2. Bureau of vital statistics,
3. Marriage Hall, 4. Library atrium

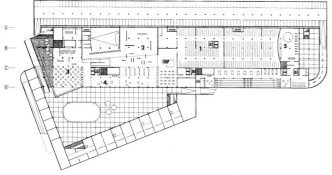

Level –1 1. Library, 2. Exhibition gallery, 3. Café, 4. Restaurant, 5. Brasserie

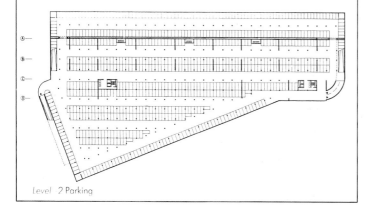

Level –2 Parking

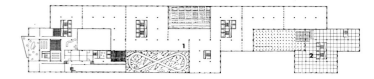

Level +6 (Technical services: 1. Offices, 2. Computer room

Level +3 1. City Hall reception, 2. Library, 3. Municipal archives

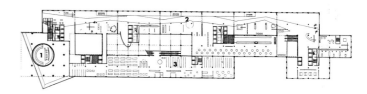

Level +2 1. Attorney general's office, 2. Commercial gallery, 3. Library

Level +1 1. Vital statistics bureau, 2. Library services

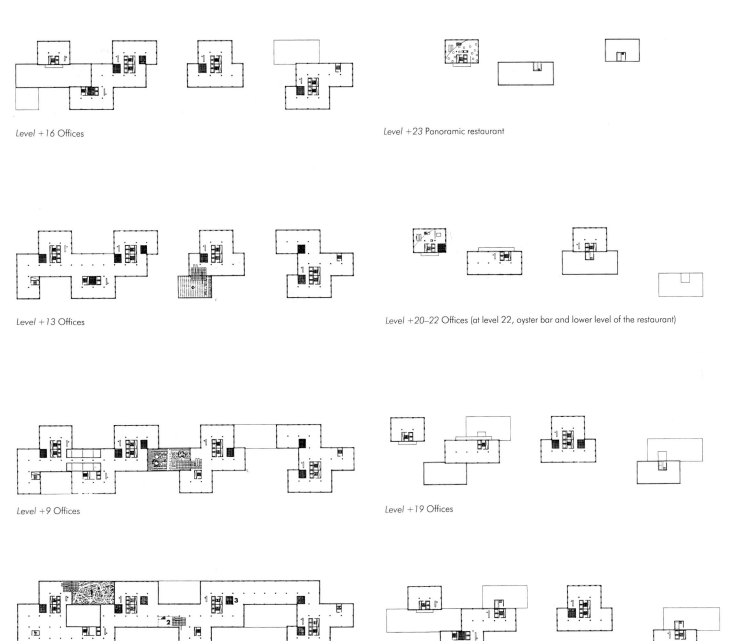

Level +16 Offices

Level +23 Panoramic restaurant

Level +13 Offices

Level +20–22 Offices (at level 22, oyster bar and lower level of the restaurant)

Level +9 Offices

Level +19 Offices

Level +7 Offices: 1. Garden, 2. Lounge, 3. Service boxes

Level +17–18 Offices

Office Complex
Frankfurt 1989

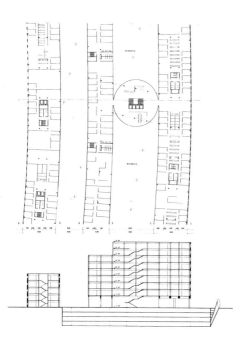

Landscape

This administrative complex houses at least 15,000 people and thus becomes a veritable *quartier*—even, in the context of the airport, an entirely separate city. The organizational form, at once the most efficient and the most humane, arises from encircling the existing buildings with two or three rings. In this way, the elements traditionally constituting a city (streets, parks, courtyards, gardens, and so on) were developed.

In spite of the enormity of the built masses, the ring concept has the advantage of creating an almost picturesque intimacy, while at the same time this expressive "form" finds its justification among the other forms composing the landscape of the airport.

Siting

The *exterior landscaped ring* is divided into courtyards planted to resemble the essence of agriculture: fields of wheat and sunflowers, vineyards, orchards, etc. (a bit of Ernst May's image of New Frankfurt). The *intermediate ring* takes the form of a street. It is this ring that provides the principal entrances to the various groups of offices. Cafeterias, boutiques, and other services for the 15,000 employees are located at regular intervals along this ring.

The *central plaza*, which serves to integrate the existing buildings with the new ones, becomes a small forest, a concentration of green at the heart of the project.

The office rings

The three rings of offices are largely different and allow for diverse uses. To the north, along the highway, is the longest building, composed of two rings linked by a series of towers bringing together the indi-

vidual vertical distributions. On the south side, a portico is planted in front of the rings housing the important public offices. To avoid a labyrinthine circulation, a north-south axis, linked in the south to the road connection, crosses the three rings and unites the principal circulation systems. It also links the two existing buildings and creates an entrance to the vast recreational spaces comprising a restaurant and other public facilities (gymnasia, swimming pools, etc.) projected for the roof of the existing canteen.

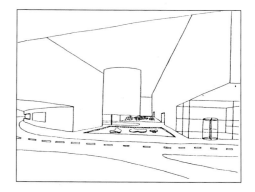

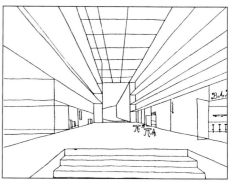

Above

Detail of plan with respective section

Right

Studies of different environments

Site plan of the complex within the system
of roads, and a view of the model

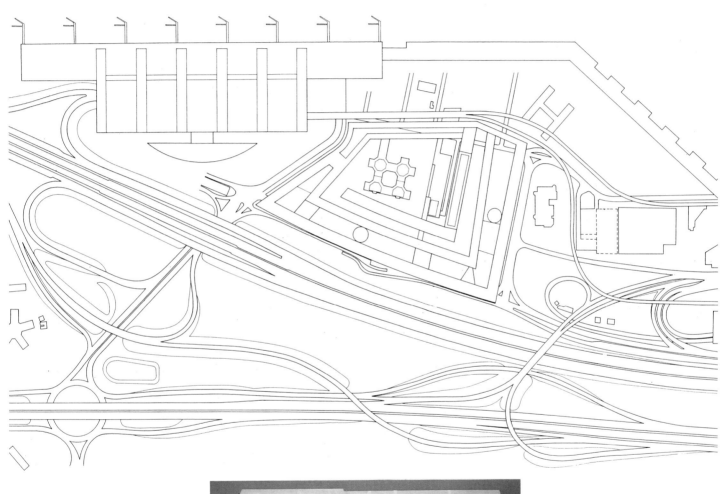

Below, from top to bottom

Plan at 6.20m

North facade, along the highway

East-west section along the exterior ring

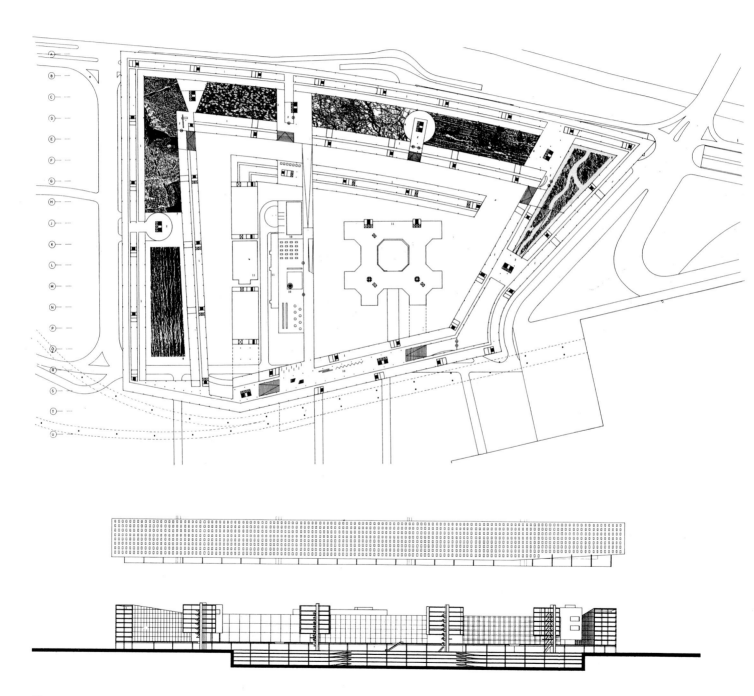

Below, from top to bottom

Plan of the office floor with the existing office
building at center and an existing cafeteria on
the north-south connection, whose roof
supports a restaurant and swimming pool

South facade with portico

East-west section

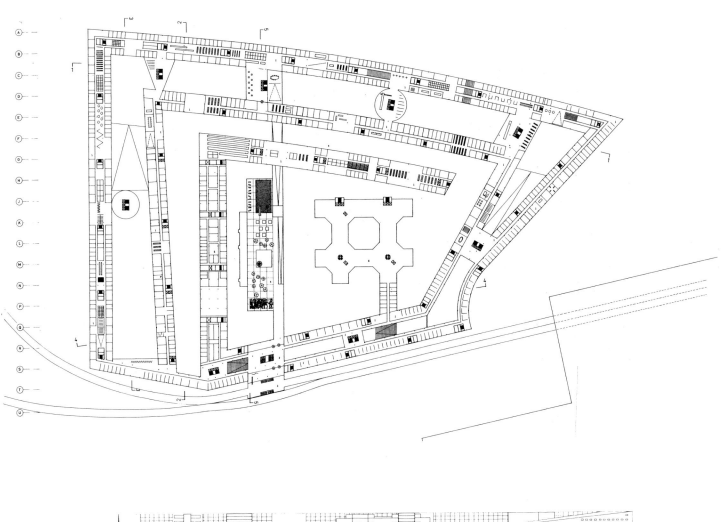

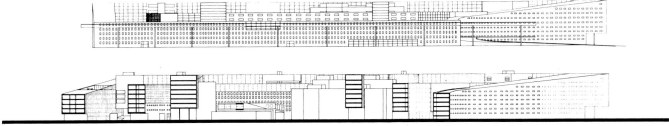

Agadir Convention Center
Morocco 1990

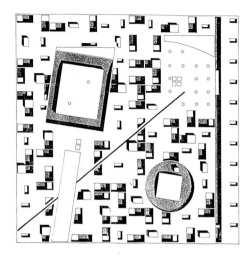

Using Agadir's street grid to determine the shape and plan of this architectural project would have interfered with any effort to conserve the spirit of modern Morocco. It would have been equally self-defeating to fall back on the concept of a large, monumental structure.

Our project should be considered as a single building "cut" into two sections, a roof and a base, determined and differentiated by a larger urban "room," or space, a covered square adjacent to the beach, overlooking the ocean in one direction and a eucalyptus grove in the other. An integral part of the seashore setting, the sand reaches and flows around the upper portion of the square. Near the main entryways and terraces, a space engendered by the shapes of the landscape itself creates, through a set of framing structures, an area that is sheltered from the wind. The rooms of a single storey, each with its own patio, dominate—with the S-curve of the facade—the glassed-in "square."

Two types of accommodations were built: one type is a two-storey living area overlooking a patio; the other type extends around a patio, with a kitchen and bath separating the living room from the bedroom.

The convention center is situated on the ground floor, in the base structure. We saw this as a challenge that called for the development of an original form of architectural expression which, while meeting the demands of the larger program, would also harmonize with the beauty of the setting. The flowing curves of the dunes are echoed in the depressions and rises of the base, which are in turn reflected on the upper, residential floor. Thus, the perception of the square is linked with the correspondence between above and below. The inside surfaces are made up of ribbed structures and decorative shapes. The upper floor rests on pillars that vary in weight, width, and height. The building is given stability by the intersection between the two parts and by the thickness of the pillars. A network of ancillary connections links the pillars and the upper beams, making the building particularly resistant to earthquakes. The outer masonry, sheathed in local stone —processed or in the natural state—gives the building a rocky appearance.

The convention center will be surrounded by hotels and clubs, which will dot the landscape like pieces of sculpture. Swimming pool, solarium, and tennis courts will be set in the shade of the eucalyptus trees and upon the sand.

Two other hotels are planned as linear structures facing the park, set on the steepest section of the entire area. Their roofs will serve as a public square, edging the coastal road. Lanes and narrow roads will connect the hotels, beach, woods, and city— thus, the entire area becomes a special part of the urban fabric, set in nature.

The ultimate effect, created by the concave and convex domes, the "forest" of pillars, the light shafts, is that of a modern version of Islamic spatial construction; this is seen as well in the choice of materials: polished concrete, mosaics, tiles, and so on.

There is a multi-level parking structure, set in a U-shape around the building. A sand bank gives the complex a certain degree of independence and isolation.

The concrete base and the upper floor were formed on-site, composed of individual shell sections, using sand as a natural mold.

Facing page

Roof plan

Below

Perspective views of the convention center

Bottom

Site plan

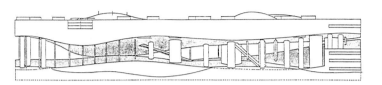

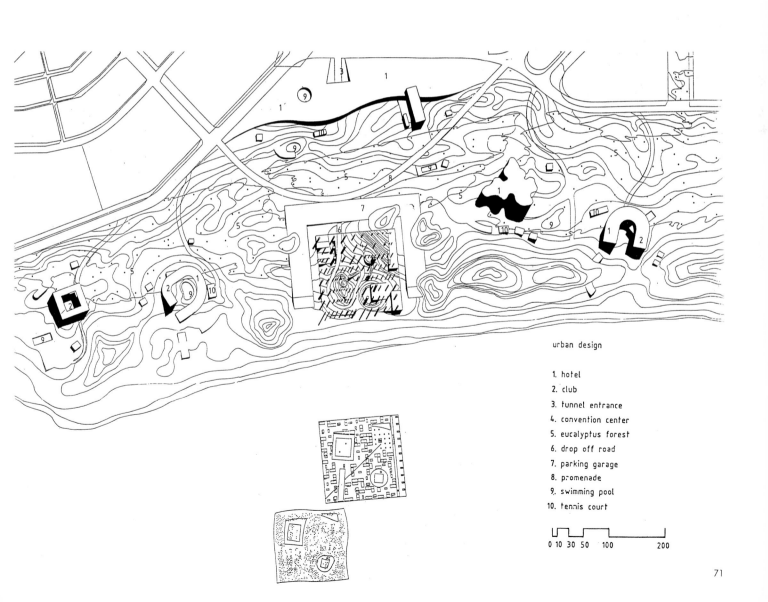

urban design

1. hotel
2. club
3. tunnel entrance
4. convention center
5. eucalyptus forest
6. drop off road
7. parking garage
8. promenade
9. swimming pool
10. tennis court

0 10 30 50   100   200

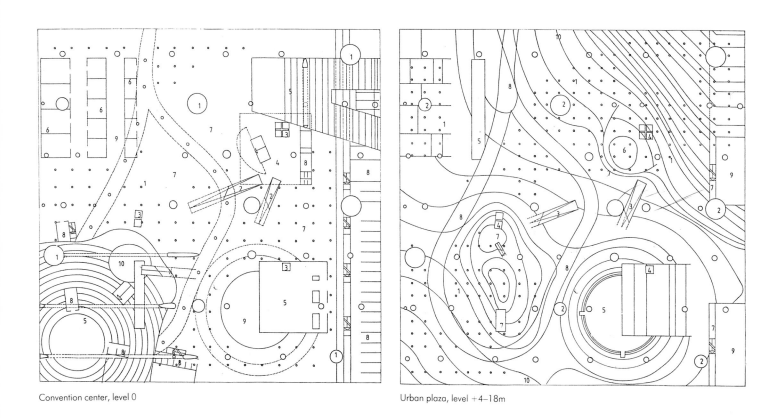

Convention center, level 0

Urban plaza, level +4–18m

Section through A

Section through B

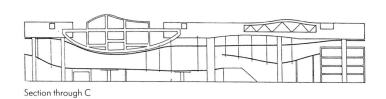

Section through C

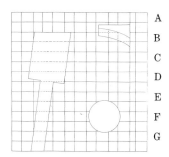

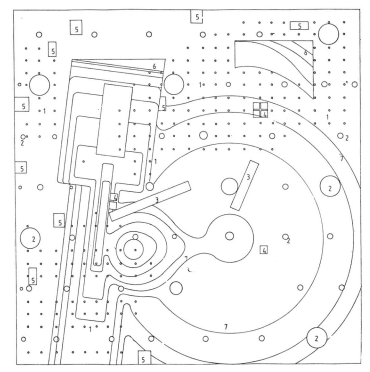

Roof, level +10–18m

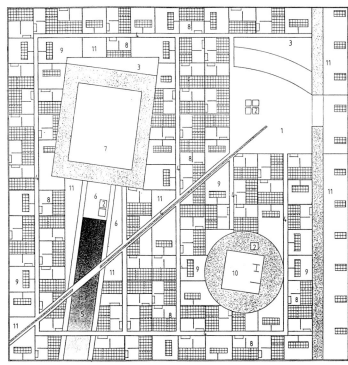

Hotel, level +20m

Section through E

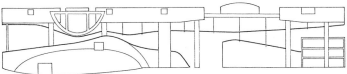

Section through F

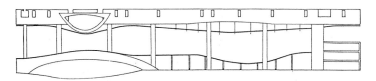

Section through G

Various room typologies of the hotel
shown distributed in plans and
corresponding sections

Horizontal Projects

IJ-plein

Amsterdam-North 1980–1989

Left

The IJ-plein site before the basin was filled

Right

View of the area after completion of the project

Amsterdam is divided into two parts: the center of town is located south of the IJ (formerly the front of the port); north of the water (what was once the sea) is Amsterdam-North, an almost village-like zone isolated from the sea by a belt of docks and shipyards. Since the port was displaced to the west, its lands are gradually becoming available for housing.

This project is a proposal for the part of this zone closest to the center. Its implementation is complicated by the presence of an abandoned dock in its midst.

The first part of the project involves filling in this dock: in principal, new buildings could be built on the resultant geological "fault."

Another obstacle is the path of a tunnel linking the two halves of Amsterdam.

The residential quarter immediately to the north is absolutely typical. It is called Vogel-Dorp, which means "the village of birds"—the streets of this small urban development zone are all named after birds.

The site's tension lies exactly in the dichotomy between an almost village-like context and an effectively central location, between the desire to maintain a low scale for the buildings and the pressure to build. Since the existing housing actually faces the IJ and from it derives a strikingly humble quality, it seems important not to completely discount it. A central lawn divides the site into two halves, providing a viewing corridor for the existing houses: to the east sits a new version of the village, with streets perpendicular to the water; to the west lies a series of taller buildings, a village of apartment houses placed in checkerboard fashion, assuring a view toward the city and the

water. At the center of the "village," a triangular plaza reflects and inverts the organization of the other "village of birds."

This experiment is up to this point unique for us, to the extent to which we are planners and not architects, and so, as a consequence, the project must remain schematic. This rests on the fact that, when dealing with social housing, there is no money for details; therefore the organization and siting must provide the basis for interest.

Urban studies of IJ-plein showing the
various modern projects for the site

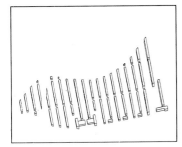

W. Gropius, Dammerstock, 1927–1928

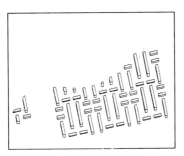

Rotterdam CIAM Group, Pendrecht, 1949

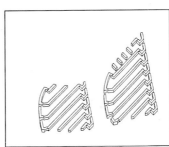

E. May, Riedhof, 1927–1930

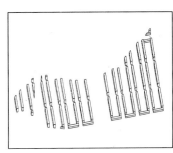

L. Hilberseimer, urban plan, 1923

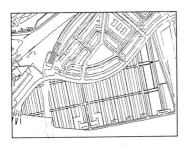

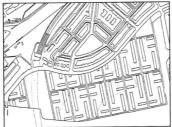

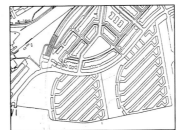

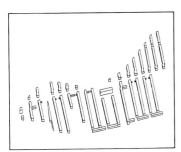

M. Stam, Hellerhof, 1921–1930

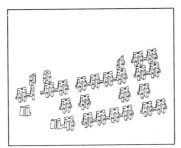

J. Duiker, study for high-rise housing, 1930

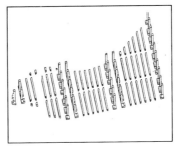

J. Duiker, project for the third CIAM

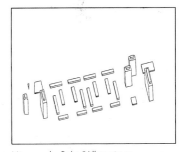

Mies van der Rohe/Hilberseimer,
La Fayette Park, 1955

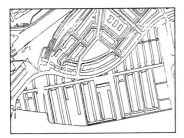

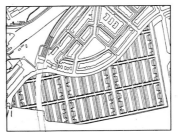

Left

General axonometric of OMA's

proposed structures

Right

Plan of the western sector

showing landscape designs

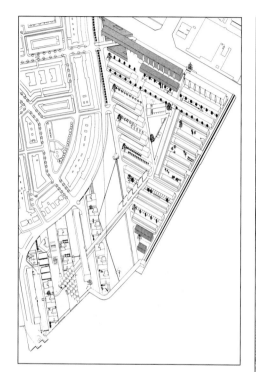

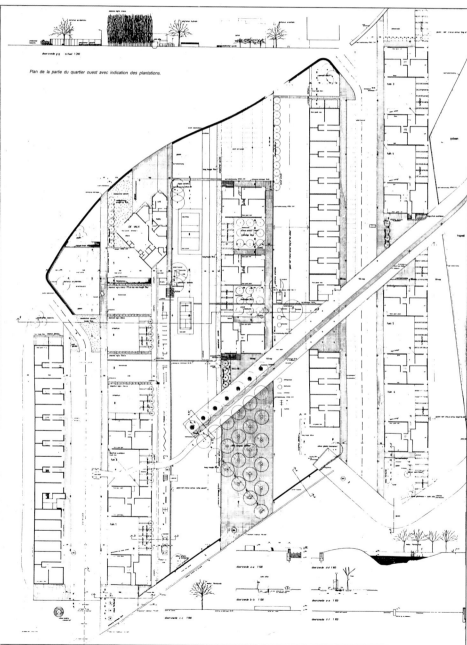

Below

Plans of ground floor and second through fifth

floors of the apartment building

Facing page

View of the apartment building and street passage

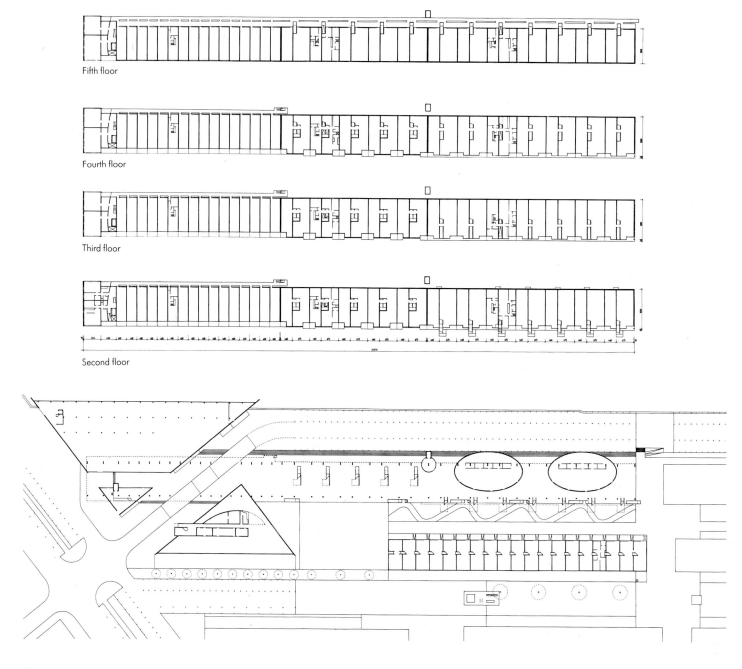

Fifth floor

Fourth floor

Third floor

Second floor

Views of the facade along the canal and
of the internal street between the two
apartment buildings

Exploded axonometric of the two apartment
buildings showing various dwelling types

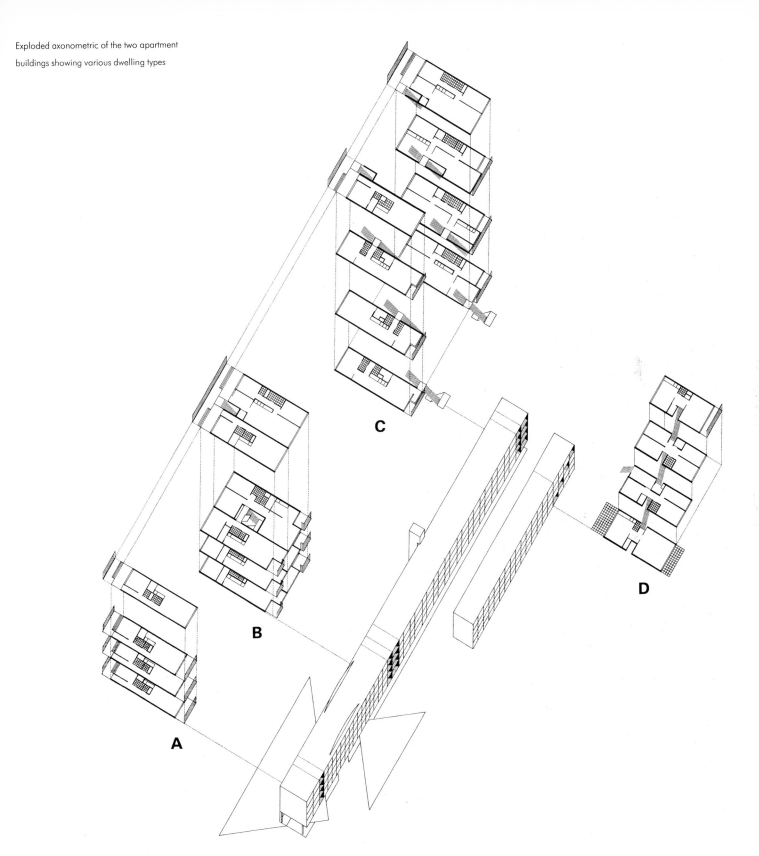

A

B

C

D

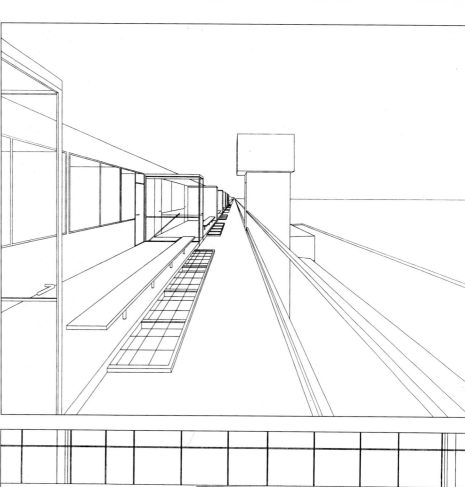

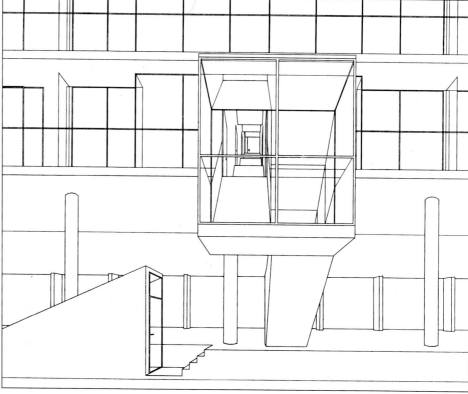

Detailed plans showing apartment typologies

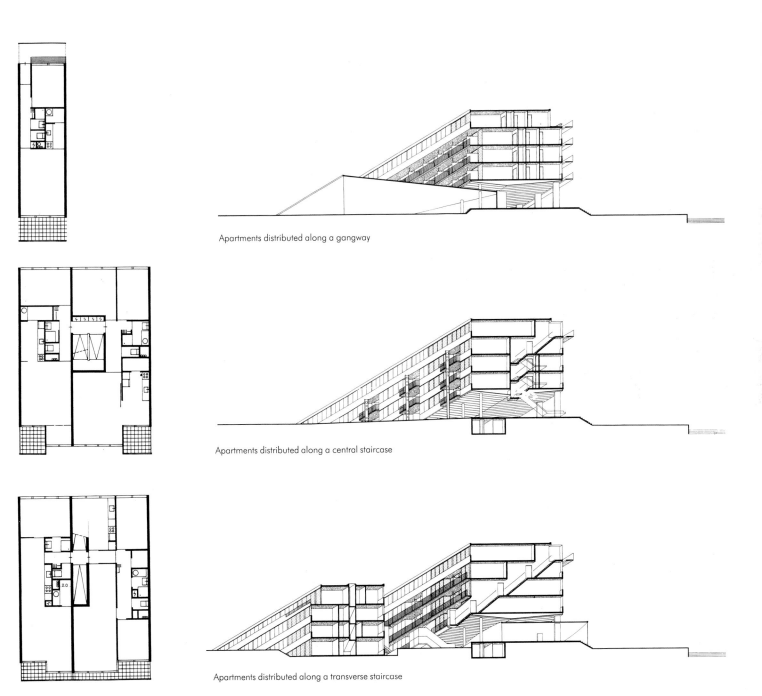

Apartments distributed along a gangway

Apartments distributed along a central staircase

Apartments distributed along a transverse staircase

Parc de la Villette
Paris 1982–1983

Initial Hypothesis

As the diagram reveals, the site of la Villette is too small, and the program for the Park de la Villette too large, to create a park in the recognizable sense of the word. A conventional park is a replica of nature serviced by a minimal number of facilities that ensure its enjoyment; the program of the Park de la Villette extends like a dense forest of social instruments across the site. At this stage it would be nonsense to design a detailed park. We have read the program as a suggestion, a provisional enumeration of desirable ingredients that is not definitive. It is safe to predict that during the life of the Park, the program will undergo constant change and adjustment. The more the Park works, the more it will be in a state of revision. Its "design" should therefore be

the proposition of a "method" that combines architectural specificity with programmatic indeterminacy. That is, we see this scheme not simply as a design, but as a tactical proposal to derive maximum benefit from the implantation of a number of activities on the site—incorporating the use of nature—in the most efficient and explosive manner, while at the same time offering a (relatively) stable aesthetic experience.

The underlying principle of programmatic indeterminacy as a basis of the formal concept allows any shift, modification, replacement, or substitution to occur without damaging the initial hypothesis. The essence of the competition becomes, therefore, how to orchestrate on a metropolitan field the most dynamic coexistence of x, y, and z activities and to generate through their mutual interference a chain reaction of new, unprecedented events; or, how to design a Social Condenser, based on horizontal congestion, that is the size of a park.

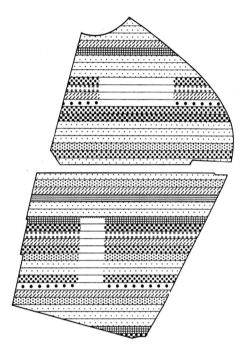

The Bands

In the first primordial gesture the whole site is subdivided in a series of parallel bands—running east-west—that can accommodate, in principle, zones of the major programmatic categories: the theme gardens, half of the playgrounds, discovery gardens, etc.

In this way, concentration or clustering of any particular programmatic component is avoided; the band can be distributed across the site partly at random, partly according to a logic derived from the existing characteristics of the site.

This tactic of layering creates the maximum length of "borders" between the largest number of different programmatic components and thereby guarantees a maximum

permeability of each programmatic band by all the others, and—through this interference—the largest number of programmatic mutations.

The direction of the bands is chosen so that the dominant elements already on the site—the Science Museum and the Great Hall—are incorporated in the system: the Museum as an extra-wide band (which could itself be divided in analogous thematic bands), the Hall as an incidental, covered part of another series of bands running through it. The strips are based on standard dimensions—a basic width of 50m subdivisible in increments of 5, 10, 25, or 40m—to facilitate change and replacement without disruption, and to create fixed points for the infrastructure. Nature—whether in the form of the thematic or discovery gardens, or even "real"

Left

The point grid, distributing atomized

installations across the site

Right

The Boulevard and the Promenade

traversing the site

nature—is also be treated as program. Blocks or screens of trees and the various gardens will act like different planes of a stage set: they will convey the illusion of different landscapes, of depth, without offering the substance.

The layering is not unlike a high-rise building, with its superimposed floors all capable of supporting different programmatic events, yet all contributing to a summation that is more than the accumulation of parts.

Point Grids or Confetti

Excluded from the treatment above are relatively small-scale elements that occur across the site with some frequency: kiosks (11), playgrounds (the 50% that is not organized in bands but divided into 15 separate units), sales kiosks (30), refreshment bars (15), and

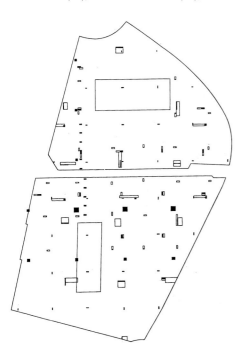

picnic areas (five large and 25 smaller ones). Their distribution, in the form of different point grids across the site, is established mathematically on the basis of their desirable frequency. The frequency calculation was relative to the available area (zone A), the total area per service asked for, an assessment of the optimum number of points required across the site, and the need for distribution across either the whole or part of the site. The formula for determining the dimensions of each point grid then becomes:

$$\sqrt{\frac{A - a}{x}}$$

where A is the area of Zone A, a is the required area of the facility, and x is the number of points to be distributed.

Since the Park as a whole is divided in bands, it follows that the elements on the point grids occur each time in different zones, thereby both acquiring and influencing the character of the "host" zone; i.e., a kiosk in zone x is different from a kiosk in zone y, even if they are the same design. The occasional proximity of the various elements distributed as part of the different grids leads to random and accidental "clusterings" that give every constellation of points its unique configuration and character. Besides their autonomy, which gives a recognizable identity to each facility at fixed intervals, and their intention to be absorbed by and thus affect their locality, their projection on the site creates unity through fragmentation. Although small, the point grids consist of compositional permutations of a series of identical, strong, colorful, recognizable elements that litter the site—as if after a pinpoint bombardment of small meteorites—with tectonic confetti.

Access and Circulation

The access and circulation system nourishes all the episodes of the Park and ensures their most intense exploitation. It consists of two major elements: the first of these, the Boulevard, runs north-south, systematically intersecting all the bands at right angles; it also directly connects the major architectural components of the Park—the Museum and Baths in the north, the City of Music and Great Hall in the south. Of its total width of 25m, 5m are covered.

The Promenade, complementary to the Boulevard, is generated through the identification and subsequent demarcation—in the form of plazas—of certain significant cross-sections as they are fortuitously created through the interaction of the bands. These "sites within the site" are further equipped

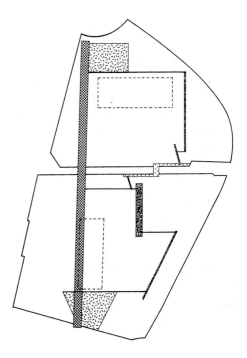

with facilities such as small amphitheaters, seating, chess tables, tribunes, puppet theaters, roller-skating surfaces, etc. Each one also accommodates a greenhouse, so that a journey along the Promenade will represent a fragmented visit to them all.

The plaza-like elements of the Promenade are connected by the east-west paths of the strips: along the Canal de l'Ourcq, Boulevard and Promenade are formally joined through a riverside ambulatory, so that the circulation system forms a figure 8.

The Boulevard represents the 24-hour part of the program: all-night facilities are located on or along it. Even when the rest of the Park is closed, the Boulevard—combining the glare of neon with the lure of a never-ending public life along its perimeter—will be a major metropolitan element in the texture of Paris, a late 20th-century equivalent of the Arcades. The entrances of the Promenade coincide with (and control) the opening of the Park itself.

The Final Layer

The final layer is a composition of the major elements—created and "found"—that are unique or too large to be located according to mathematical rules or a system. The relative regularity and neutrality of the first three layers forms a background/context against which these elements become significant. These are intermediate-sized, unique objects such as the sphere of the Museum, the Ariane rocket, and the Rotonde des Vétérinaires, that have been placed according to organizing lines extrapolated from the context or absorbed, where possible, as part of the intentions of the Park.

The large-scale composition consists, furthermore, of the two major "givens"—

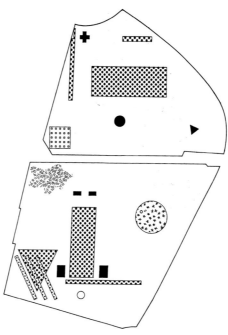

the Museum and the Great Hall—amplified by the circular forest and a series of architectural interventions that help to define the boundaries of the Park without necessarily coinciding with its perimeter: a reception square and Baths in the north, which counteract the dominance of the Museum in that sector; the Music Zone in the south, which, together with the other major elements, helps to define an entrance zone; a Facade Building that displays the entrances to both the Boulevard and the Promenade and accommodates all the facilities necessary for managing the Park.

Connections and Elaborations

There are two major areas of interface between the Park and the streets of Paris: the Rotonde des Vétérinaires in the north and to the east the large square vestibule of the

Museum.

To extend the presence of the Park to the Rue Jean Jaures, we suggest a departure from the program in zone C. We propose to locate the City of Music in the wedge-shaped area between the city and the new Boulevard, east of the Great Hall.

The symbol of the City of Music suggests the triangular mass, intersected by three "beams" that extend to the street to reinforce the entrance to the Park. The triangle would contain the auditoria; the three "beams," on pilotis, could represent the three institutions: Conservatory, Research Institute, Music Museum. In the north the facilities of the City of Music can extend as far as necessary and merge with the activities of the Park.

The City of Music forms the southern boundary together with the Facade Building: from the entrance to the Boulevard, the various information centers, the police, PTT, the fire brigade, restaurants, and the entrance to the Promenade.

The railway line to the Butte is transformed into a vegetal connection between the two formal languages of the Park: the rectilinear and the curvilinear.

The entertainment zone directly behind the Facade Building consists of an inclined amphitheatrical plane equipped for open-air performances, the circus, etc. It continues underneath the Great Hall—where it accommodates the major exhibition area—to the City of Music.

The Astronomical Garden not only incorporates "indigestible" givens such as the sphere of the Museum, trying to make sense of them, but also includes two major urban connections: one to the west via the lock in the Canal Saint Denis, and a second that extends across the Périphérique into the suburban parts of Paris. In addition the Astronomical Garden consists of two elements; the first is a *sequence of squares* (40 x 40m) running from the Canal Saint Denis to the leather-tanning hall on the other side of the Périphérique, intersected by a *line* that runs across the band from the locks to the roof of the Great Hall, first in the form of a bridge, then a cable and chairlift, and then a parabolic ramp.

Each square in this sequence contains exhibits for the Museum of Science: an ocean basin with bathyscaphe, the Ariane launching pad, permanent sheltered exhibition space, the Hemispherical Hall, radio telescope, observatories, and the Antennae Forest. A section of the Périphérique is caught in this band as an exhibit.

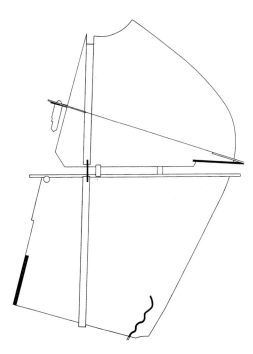

On the line of the cable and the chairlift, the planets of the solar system are arranged according to their distances from the sun. In this constellation the Hemispherical Hall becomes Saturn and is provided with a fluorescent ring. The sun coincides with the Boulevard and is represented by the sundial that also acts as a terminal for the cable and chairlift. In the east, the cable and the chairlift end at the cube-tearoom, built on top of the leather-tanning hall.

The cube, the pyramid-greenhouse, the sphere, and the other tall objects on the band and the lines, create a Newtonian skyline along the Canal de l'Ourcq against the background of the Museum. This landscape is intensified by the representation of the orbit of the celestial bodies in the form of trees and hedges.

The theme garden elaborated is the Media Strip: a production area west of the Great Hall, and a "sets" garden to the east of it. The Media Garden offers opportunities for the production—at the amateur level—of films, video, and radio, so that visitors and local residents may themselves manipulate this passive component of modern life. The "sets" garden exploits the scenic possibilities offered in this location by two glasshouses and the Circular Forest. Continuous transformations of this fabricated landscape are made possible by a rigging area, turning this whole section into an accelerated and intensified model of the park as a whole.

Demonstration

Our submission for the first stage showed an adherence to the program and to the primacy of its social dimension. We imagined the cohabitation of a vast number of human activities on the site, combined to

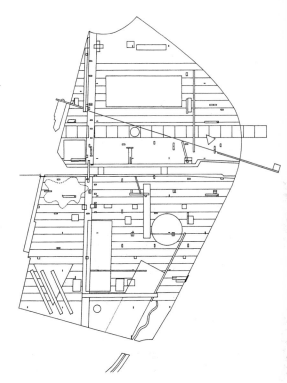

engender a park.

In this further clarification for the second stage, we describe in detail the landscape generated by this organization. Having explained how it works we now demonstrate what it looks like.

To insert the park in its urban environment requires extremely concrete data, and so we have abstained from elaborating on the interface of park and city. Instead we concentrate here on the most crucial element to the park's success: its central region or "torso" (which is also developed in the model). If the framework of our project is assembled as a programmatic two-dimensional tapestry, then its third (spatial) dimension is given by the component "nature." The spatial exploration of the original concept leads directly to a description of this "natural" dimension.

Principles

The Park is a *mise en scène* of three different categories of nature.

One: Regions in which the program itself is nature, i.e., expanses where the vegetal dominates (thematic gardens, didactic gardens, play-prairies, etc.). Often these have been regrouped to invest large aggregate areas with the *transposed image* of fields.

Two: Screens of trees, parallel to the bands that define the zones, which at the same time create a series of successive landscapes. This east-west marking of the zones in the form of arboreal screens (differing in height, species, transparency, density, and homogeneity), produces *curtains* as in the theater, which together act as "*sliding landscapes*."

The trees that make up these screens are combined to maximize the effect: for example, the natural dominant type in a row such as *acer* (the species of the maple tree variety) is mixed with its *cultivar* series, and the *clone* opposes to the individual parent plant. This sequential juxtaposition, by displaying the variety of each species, has a didactic as well as an aesthetic purpose.

Two modes of perception emerge from this arrangement: together, seen in the layered north-south perspective, these screens interweave and suggest the presence of a tree mass (about 6,000 trees) covering the entire site. In the inverse east-west views, these screens frame open surfaces, like "fields." Occasional breaches open up vistas. This play of enclaves and connections produces the effect of contracting or expanding the apparent depth of field. This strategy is adopted to make the space between the

Museum and the canal participate in the organization of the Park's center.

The opposition between these diverse perceptions is further exploited by the major axes of circulation, the Promenade and the Boulevard. There is opposition between the displayed and the hidden: the goal of the Promenade is continually deflected. Conversely, the course of the Boulevard unfolds without surprises, the progressive stages along its passage are deliberately explicit. The Promenade is surprise, the Boulevard certainty.

Three: Vegetal elements conceived at the scale of the major architectural elements on the site, of which they form the counterpoint. The Linear Forest, south of the Canal de Ourcq, and the Circular Forest at the center of the Park, have a dialectic correspondence: from the natural to the artificial, from the solid to the hollow, from the evergreen to the deciduous. This opposition provides the entire spectrum of possible variations on the theme "image of the forest." The Linear Forest forms a backdrop against which all vegetal and architectural components in the southern part of the Park stand out in relief. In section though the mixed assortment of trees, shrubs, and evergreen climbers, it assumes a maximum impermeability. The whole is planted in a free quasi-natural pattern. Occasional cuts through its continuous mass ensure visual connections with important elements on the other side of the canal. In this respect the Linear Forest acts as a filter to the Museum, the mass of which it controls, while heightening its accents. By locating this illusion of forest on the axis of the Place Stalingrad, by providing a row of chestnut trees, poised in equilibrium on the opposite bank of the canal, and finally, by conserving the monumental bridge in a verdant version, we advertise an *emblem* of park that can be deciphered from Paris.

The Circular Forest is raised on a three-metre socle that accentuates its entrances. Where the Linear Forest is a catalogue of natural features, the Circular Forest represents the *forest as program*, compressing in an artificial way the sensations and associations linked with the idea of forest. It is a Forest Machine or, at least, a Forest Building. The Linear Forest acts as a dense *mass*, the Circular Forest is an *interior*. Its trees—cypresses alternating with Lebanese Cedars—produce the effect of majestic rows of columns covered by a dark green roof of vegetation, which in the day calibrates the rays of light penetrating from the sky and at night is artificially illuminated from the ground.

A marble floor traverses the forest. To the columns of trees are added the smoke wisps rising from a number of campfires, hollowed out randomly on this perfect surface. An ambulatory, like the walk-round of traditional fortifications, runs along the periphery of the socle. Proceeding from afar, carried by the aqueduct, the water's course is progressively transformed; beginning as a river, it changes into jets that spring up to the forest and are collected in a basin that becomes a canal, and finally turns into a cascade, with the sunken gardens accompanying it forming a clearing in the forest. Independently of the three systems of nature, the landscape incorporates a series of anti-categorical elements: scattered on the site, virgin nature islets, where single trees or small groups grow freely. These islets constitute an archipelago of fragments exploded from the traditional romantic park: geometric splashes of color in the grass and on the ground, applied like a kind of floral wallpaper, these color speckles spring up in response to the rhythm of the seasons, intense and ephemeral apparitions, almost a mirage.

Developing the landscape

In accordance with the principle of the useful at the service of the aesthetic, the landscaping should be conceived as the sum of the infrastructural interventions required. At La Villette the soil is often sterile, and our vegetal strategy asks for fertility. We shall take advantage of the necessity to transport new soil to the site and turn this into a supplementary theme for our project. To this end we aim at two objectives: to differentiate the nature of the varied soil strata required (healthy soil, peat, etc.) by juxtaposing vegetal sets that would not be possible in a homogeneously fertile ground; and by raising or hollowing out the different layers of soil, to show clearly these diverse strata in elevation and so further accentuate the third dimension of the landscape.

Conclusion

Finally, we would maintain that at no time did we presume to have produced a *designed* landscape. We have confined ourselves to devising a framework capable of absorbing an endless series of further meanings, extensions or intentions, without entailing compromises, redundancies, or contradictions. Our strategy is to confer on the simple the dimension of adventure.

When the useful coincides with the poetic, reality cannot but stick to the conceptual.

Left

Diagram of the central area with

its programmatic bands

Right

Diagram of landscaping elements

Facing page

General plan of the functional bands

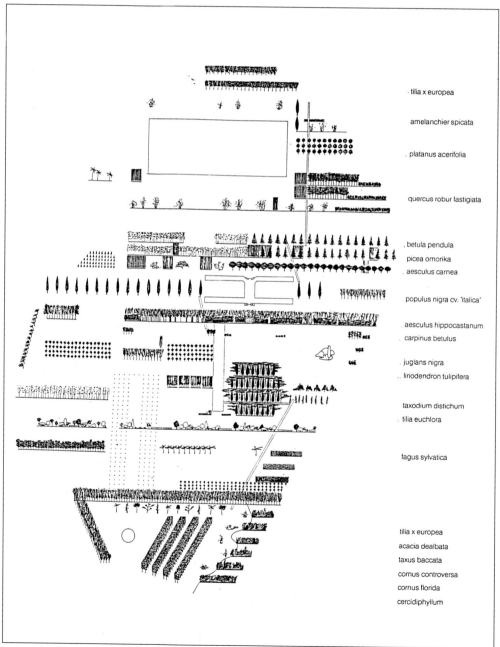

. tilia x europea

amelanchier spicata

. platanus acerifolia

quercus robur fastigiata

. betula pendula
picea omorika
. aesculus carnea

populus nigra cv. 'italica'

. aesculus hippocastanum
. carpinus betulus

. juglans nigra
.. liriodendron tulipifera

taxodium distichum
. tilia euchlora

fagus sylvatica

tilia x europea
acacia dealbata
taxus baccata
cornus controversa
cornus florida
cercidiphyllum

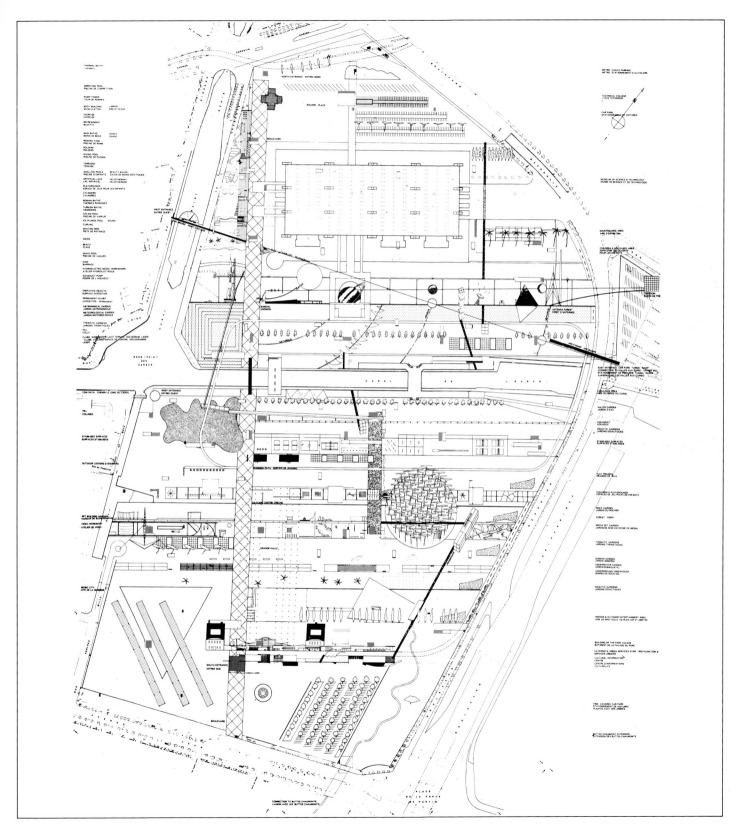

THERMAL BATHS
THERMES

SPRINTING POOL
PISCINE DE COMPETITION

PUMP TOWER
TOUR DE POMPES

BODY-BUILDING   LIBRARY
MUSCULATION   BIBLIOTHEQUE

EXERCISE
EXERCISE

REFRESHMENT
BUVETTE

MUD BATHS   DANCE
BAINS DE BOUE   DANSE

ROWING TANK
PISCINE DE RAME

POLDERS
POLDERS

DIVING POOL
PISCINE DE PLONGE

TERRASSE
TERRASSE

SHALLOW POOLS   BEAUTY SALON
PISCINE D'ENFANTS   SALON DE SOINS ESTHETIQUES

ARTIFICIAL LAKE   HELIOTHERAPY
LAC ARTIFICIEL   HELIOTHERAPIE

PLAYGROUNDS
ESPACE DE JEUX POUR LES ENFANTS

CYLINDERS
CYLINDRES

ROMAN BATHS
THERMES ROMAINES

TURKISH BATHS
HAMMAMS

STEAM POOL
PISCINE DE VAPEUR

ICE PLUNGE POOL   SAUNA
CURLING

SKATING RINK
PISTE DE PATINAGE

OASIS
PLAGE

WAVE POOL
PISCINE DE VAGUES

DAM
BARRAGE

HYDROELECTRIC MODEL WORKSHOPS
ATELIER HYDROELECTRIQUE

AQUEDUCT PUMP
POMPE DE L'AQUADUC

DISPLAYED OBJECTS
SURFACE EXPOSITION

PERMANENT EXHIBIT
EXPOSITION PERMANENT

ASTRONOMICAL GARDEN
JARDIN ASTRONOMIQUE

METEOROLOGICAL GARDEN
JARDIN METEOROLOGIQUE

THEMATIC GARDENS
JARDINS THEMATIQUES

HILL
COLLE

CLUBS WORKSHOP LIGHT TERRACE HOLOGRAM LASER
CLUBS ATELIER ESPACE DE LUMIERE HOLOGRAMME LASER

TOW PATH CHEMIN LE LONG DU CANAL

HILL
COLLINES

STABILISED SURFACES
SURFACES STABILISEES

OUTDOOR LOCKERS & SHOWERS
Rue de Transmission

NET BUILDING HANGAR
HANGAR DE CHARPENTE

VIDEO WORKSHOP
ATELIER DE VIDEO

MUSIC CITY
CITE DE LA MUSIQUE

NORTH ENTRANCE ENTREE NORD

SQUARE PLACE

BOULEVARD

WEST ENTRANCE
ENTREE OUEST

SUNDIAL GNOMON

WEST ENTRANCE
ENTREE OUEST

DAYCARE CENTRE CRECHE

GRANDE HALLE

SOUTH ENTRANCE
ENTREE SUD

BOULEVARD

CONNECTION TO BUTTES CHAUMONTS
LIAISON AVEC LES BUTTES CHAUMONTS

ROND-POINT
DES
CANAUX

CANAL   DE   L'OURCQ

ANTENNA FOREST
FORET D'ANTENNES

METRO COACH PARKING
METRO STATIONNEMENT D'AUTOCARS

TECHNICAL COLLEGE
LYCEE TECHNIQUE

CAR PARK
STATIONNEMENT DE VOITURES

MUSEUM OF SCIENCE & TECHNOLOGY
MUSEE DE SCIENCE ET DE TECHNOLOGIE

MAINTENANCE AREA
AIRE D'ENTRETIEN

CHILDREN'S DISCOVERY AREA
ESPACE DE DECOUVERTE POUR LES ENFANTS

EAST ENTRANCE CAR PARK TUNNEL RAMP
(CONNECTION TO HALLES AUX CURES)
STATIONNEMENT DE POIDS LOURDS
(LIAISON AVEC LES HALLES AUX CURES)

BRIDGE AREA
AIRE DE BERGE DU CANAL

WATER GARDEN
JARDIN D'EAU

AQUADUCT
AQUADUC

DIDACTIC GARDENS
JARDINS DIDACTIQUES

STABILISED SURFACES
SURFACES STABILISEES

PLAY PRAIRIES
PRAIRIES DE JEUX

CHILDREN'S PLAYGROUNDS
ESPACES DE JEU POUR LES ENFANTS

ROCK GARDEN
JARDIN DU ROCHER

FOREST FORET

MEDIA SET GARDEN
JARDIN DE MISE EN SCENE DE MEDIA

THEMATIC GARDENS
JARDINS THEMATIQUES

SUNKEN GARDEN
JARDIN IMMERGE

UNDERWATER GARDEN
JARDIN SUBAQUATIC

UNDERGROUND GREENHOUSE
SERRES EN SOUS SOL

DIDACTIC GARDENS
JARDINS DIDACTIQUES

INDOOR & OUTDOOR ENTERTAINMENT AREA
AIRE DE SPECTACLE EN PLEIN AIR ET ABRITEE

BUILDING OF THE PARK FACADE
BATIMENT DE LA FACADE DU PARC

CATERING & URBAN SERVICES STRIP RESTAURATION &
SERVICES URBAINS

CULTURAL INFORMATION
CENTRE
CENTRE D'INFORMATIONS
CULTURELLES

TREE COVERED CAR PARK
STATIONNEMENT DE VOITURES
PLANTE AVEC DES ARBRES

BUTTES CHAUMONT EXTENSION
EXTENSION DES BUTTES CHAUMONTS

Below

Planting of the Circular Forest

Bottom

View of the Linear Forest

Right

Growth of the Linear Forest

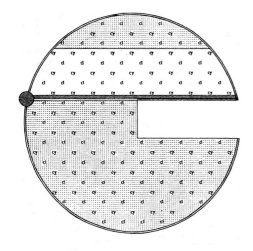

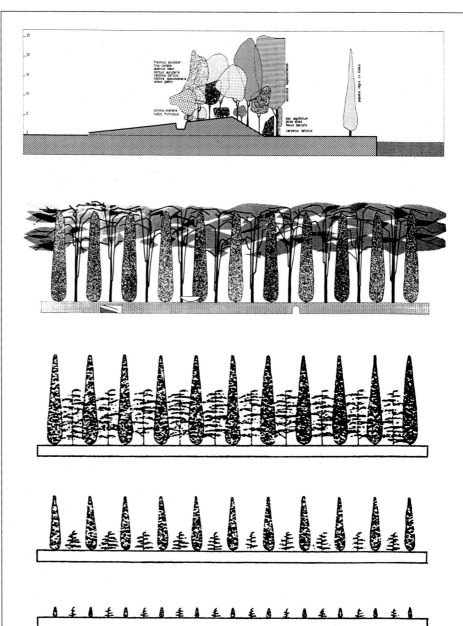

Diagram of the bands and their
designated functions
Views of the model

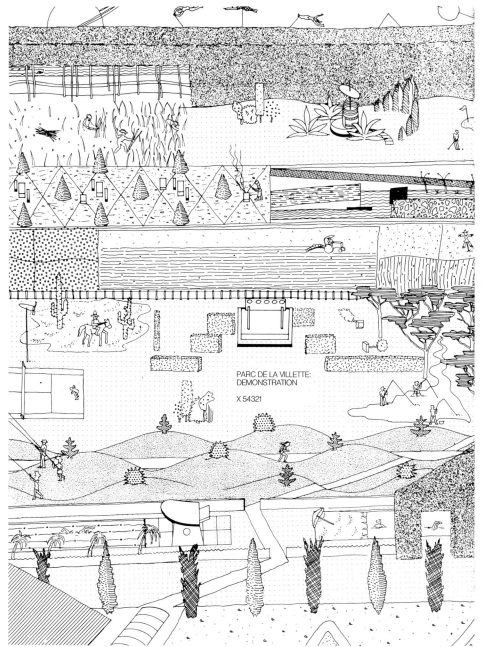

PARC DE LA VILLETTE:
DEMONSTRATION

X 54321

Universal Exposition of 1989: West Site

Paris 1983

The traditional aim, or even the function, of a Universal Exposition has been to act as a springboard for the most modern technology and to introduce this technology to the public under the most seductive conditions. In other words, the notion of Progress is necessarily linked to the notion of Future, and inevitably accompanied by the notion of the Universal Exposition. These last two concepts having largely been devalued over the past twenty years. We propose that the Exposition must contribute to their reinstatement, to effect a renaissance of the future. Since 1939, the techniques of modern presentation have necessitated less and less the services of architecture, and in many cases they are outwardly *hostile* to it. Although *buildings* or large collections of *objects* traditionally have been presented at these Expositions, they are becoming more and more *devices* in which information is presented with the most sophisticated electronic means.

These techniques place in question the very notion of "pavilion," and consequently that of a collection of trophies. The major innovation we propose for the Universal Exposition—having seen, during the last five decades, the progressive *dematerialization* caused by a growing dependence on non-architectural media—is to substitute the outmoded idea of *pavilion* and its architectural connotations, for that of *territory*, in which particular situations could be established for each nation.

A system of pure information thus would replace the mass and substance of a building—which was more and more preventing the free unfolding of illusion. This would facilitate a reduction of the gap between rich and poor nations in that it necessitates an intellectual investment rather than a financial one. In such a context, native means of communication could freely coexist with the most sophisticated technology. The formal consequence would be a more open, flexible situation.

The impressive aspect of the Exposition would reside not in the specific, recognizable structures of each nation, but in the ingenuity with which each communicated its essential characteristics with the available means. In our extreme version of this model, the entire site is divided into territories. Circulation is accomplished inside, not outside, the territories, and is assimilable into an experience close to an accelerated voyage. In the same way, the park zone is not an independent element; it is shared among the individual sites.

As a result, there will not be the traditional massing plan but a systemmatic field, a grid defining the boundaries of the territories. The entire site will become a field of information divided by invisible boundaries in which each visitor will be able to establish his own trajectory. The landscapes created during the Exposition would be on the order of electronic Potemkin villages or of a plain of artificial mirages. When the Exposition is over, the site would become a park.

Rules

For an Exposition, the ideal would be the minimum number of rules—and thus the maximum amount of freedom—sufficient to achieve the most daring expression of the initial idea. With this preliminary statement in mind, and with the establishment of the discipline-giving grid defining the individual territories, it is clear that the realization of the model must be guaranteed.

"*The Grid's two-dimensional discipline also creates undreamt-of freedom for three-dimensional anarchy. The Grid defines a new balance between control and de-control in which the city can be at the same time ordered and fluid, a metropolis of rigid chaos.*"[1] In principal, the dimensions and the programs of individual territories are themselves sufficient rules. The sole constraint is to occupy the territory and to make it accessible.

This anarchic discipline can be narrowed by the introduction of certain rules such that:

—each territory corresponding to a country constitutes a small private parcel;

—each nation exercises on its territory complete formal and programmatic control;

—each nation, inside its territory, is free to exhibit whatever it wishes;

—each nation is free to communicate its message by the means it feels most appropriate;

—the built surface must not exceed a quarter, a third, etc., of each territory; the remaining area will be dedicated to open space.

Our proposal is not a project, but a strategy to establish the program on the site.

The strategy consists of superimposing three autonomous projects:

1. The pavilions/territories;
2. The circulation and the park;
3. The complex formed by the French pavilion, administration, and services.

Three "plans" show the three autonomous projects—a fourth plan presents the resulting superimposition.

1. Taken from Rem Koolhaas, *Delirious New York* (New York: Oxford University Press, 1978): 15, referring to the Grid of Manhattan. (Ed.)

Universal Exposition of 1989: East Site

Paris 1983

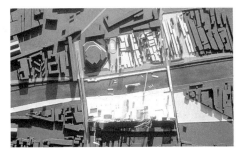

Views of models of the proposals for the east and west sites

Since information is the principal subject of the east site of the exposition, we first analyzed the various forms of its use, catalogued its means of generation and communication, and studied its potential as a supraarchitectural element capable of reinforcing or even replacing architecture . . . .

Having assembled such a catalogue, the problem of installing it on the site remained: where should we "anchor" it? What relationship should it have with built form? On the Tolbiac site in particular this point is clearly illustrated; architecture there was simply conceived as an "arena" of information. In other words, it is not a question of an exposition of various displays of information which one passively appreciates, but rather of a practical demonstration of the different aspects of information, presented across the entire site, where their qualities can be experienced first-hand.

From this "stage," "emissaries" cross the Seine to Bercy, in the form of cables, satellites, robots, and sounds, to saturate the entire site with messages, even the most remote corners. However, just as the "general headquarters" for information is found at Tolbiac but the physical activity is "based" at Bercy, the Seine becomes the means of separation and of union.

The essential quality of information is its independence of form, of containment, of architecture. It is neither bound to mass nor influenced by gravity; it is free. This project thus presents it in the form of a (partially visible) tapestry, allowing different manifestations at different points. At times, it is anchored to a specific point, but essentially it remains "in the air." In a similar manner, physical activity would be omnipresent—not as a specific, identifiable element, but rather as an interpretation of all the elements necessary to a certain level of physical activity. Like that of information, the presence of physical activity must be felt everywhere: the entire program must be interpreted in such a way as to liberate the physical potential of each element.

Remarks on the themes

It was evidently impossible in so little time to study the *content* of each theme, so we concentrated our attention on the *methods* that would permit the best communication of these themes at the desired moment and in this context. For the entire site, our strategy has been to join the useful to the thematic. Thus, when a certain means of transport was needed to connect A and B, this provided the opportunity to transmit the message Y in a fashion appropriate to the means of transport—the themes themselves became the functional links.

In this way, the means of transport themselves play an essential role: simple distribution of visitors; connection of points linked to programmatic activities; and generation of thematic itineraries throughout the site. The most extreme example is that of a visitor simultaneously equipped with a pocket computer, a miniature television, and a walkman. Armed with this arsenal, it is possible for him to compose his own thematic voyage through the exposition, responding with personal choices to the suggestions emanating from his electronic "helmet." (This recalls the red and green lines of a 3-D image: when the spectator looks only through the red gel, he does not see the red lines of the picture.) Through the medium of this "helmet," the exposition becomes an infinite spectrum of thematic lines.

West site: Models of territorial organization;
variations on the system of distributing pavilions

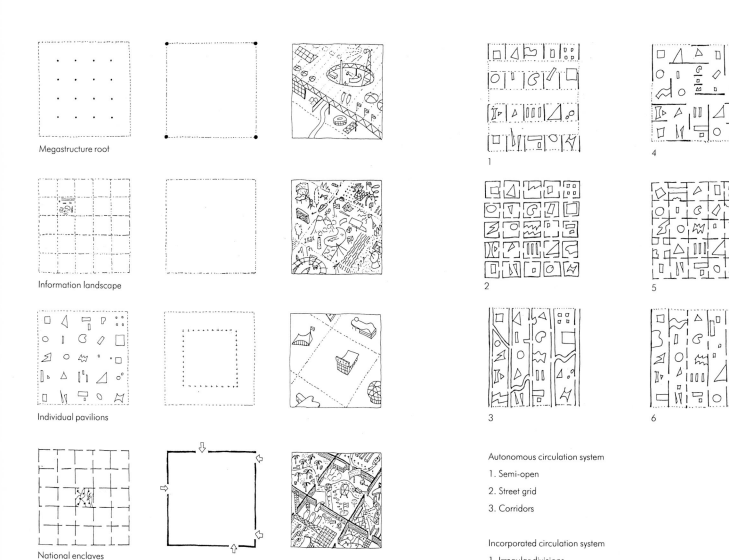

Megastructure root

Information landscape

Individual pavilions

National enclaves

1

2

3

4

5

6

Autonomous circulation system
1. Semi-open
2. Street grid
3. Corridors

Incorporated circulation system
1. Irregular divisions
2. Defined regions
3. Bands

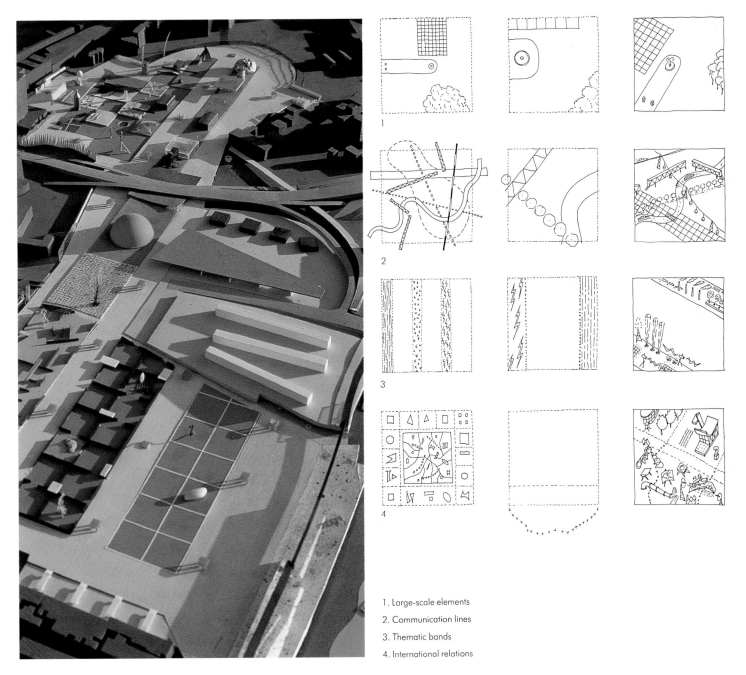

1. Large-scale elements

2. Communication lines

3. Thematic bands

4. International relations

West site: The three autonomous

projects and their superimposition

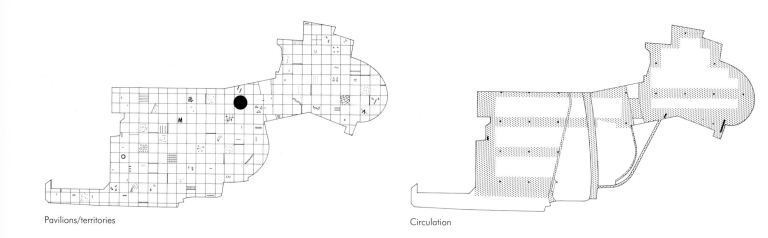

Pavilions/territories

Circulation

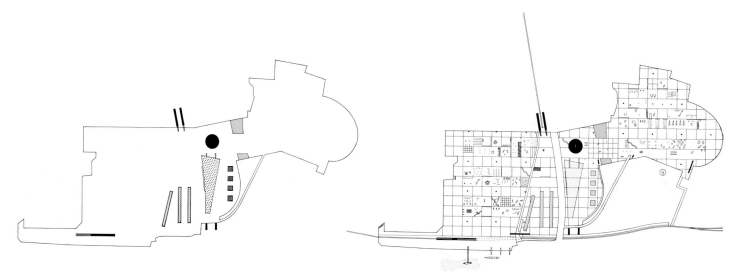

French pavilion, administration, services

Superimposition of the three projects

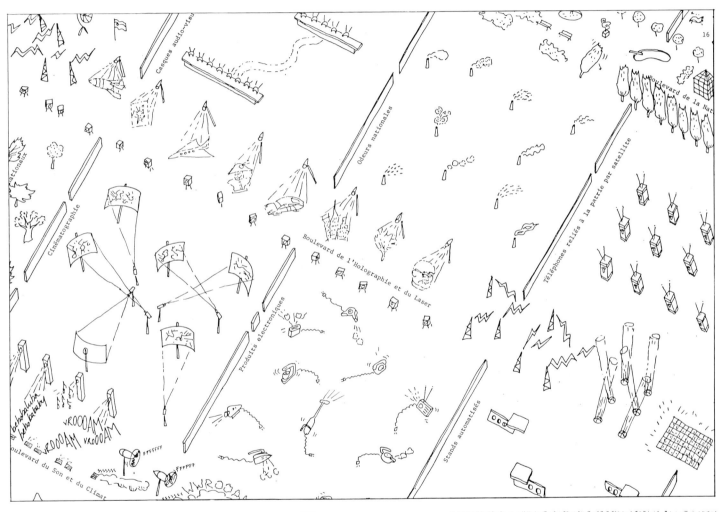

East site: Diagram illustrating the representational
methods, the transportation system, the means of
communication, and the organizational
possibilities of the program

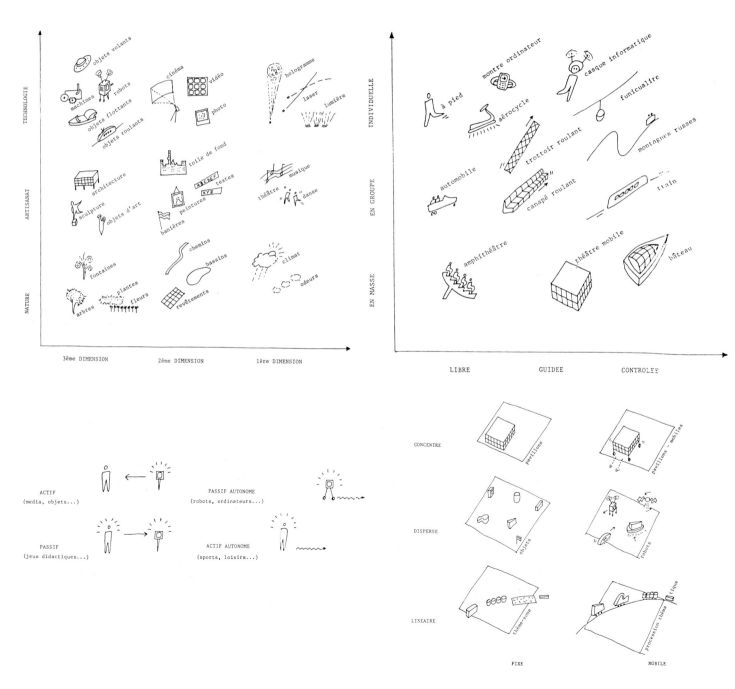

EXEMPLES DE MOYENS DE TRANSPORT	CARACTERISTIQUES DE MOUVEMENT	PASSAGERS ISOLES X GROUPES XX MASSE XXX	PAR HEURE	VITESSE ≤20 20-50 ≥50 km/h	DISTANCE récommendée par rapport au site	POSIBILITE D'USAGE PROGRAMATIQUE 10
1. MARCHER AVEC UN GUIDE ELECTRONIQUE: WALKMAN MONTRE-TELEVISION ORDINATEURS DE POCHE PRE-PROGRAMMES	"Anarchiste"	X XX XXX	∞	→	∞	Les "casques" peuvent être programmés avec un itinéraire spécifique
2. TAPIS ROULANT ESCALATOR CONVOYEUR	Circuit fixe Connection entre deux points ou à intervalles	XXX	cm 60 120 4000 8000	→	courte moyenne	Traversée d'un programme
3. TELEPHERIQUE	Circuit fixe Connection entre arrêts Application facile sur terrain difficile	X XX XXX	4000	→	moyenne longue	Eléments thématiques suspendus
4. CANAPE ROULANT	Circuit fixe Sortie et entrée multiples	XXX	10000	→	moyenne longue	Chêmin de confrontation immédiate avec le programme
5. TRAIN MONORAIL FUNICULAIRE	Circuit fixe Connection entre arrêts. Deux directions	XXX	∞	⇒	longue	Voyage d'aventure le long du tracé
6. PONTS TOURNANTS COULOIRS AMOVIBLES D'AEROPORT GRUES	Connection mobile ou fortuite de deux points	XXX	-	→	courte, moyenne	Connections fortuites Croisements d'éléments thématiques
7. MONTAGNES RUSSES	Circuit fixe et fermée Sortie et entree par une seul arrêt	XX	-	⇒	⊂⊃	La forme du tracé peut décrire des symboles. Le tracé peut faire une coupe à travers plusieurs thèmes.
8. TANKS AMPHIBIES AEROGLISSEURS SOUS-MARINS RUSSES BALLONS DIRIGEABLES	Mouvement plus ou moins anarchiste	XX	-	→	courte moyenne	Le transport lui-même est objet d'expérience
9. PAVILLONS ROULANTS ILES FLOTTANTES PONTONS	Mouvement programmé sur surface déterminée	XX	-	→	moyenne	Le transport engendre son propre programme pour être ensuite mis en scène dans une choréographie thématique
10. VOITURES AUTOBUS BATEAUX	Mouvement libre sur surface determinée	XX	-	→	∞	Itinéraire thématique programmable

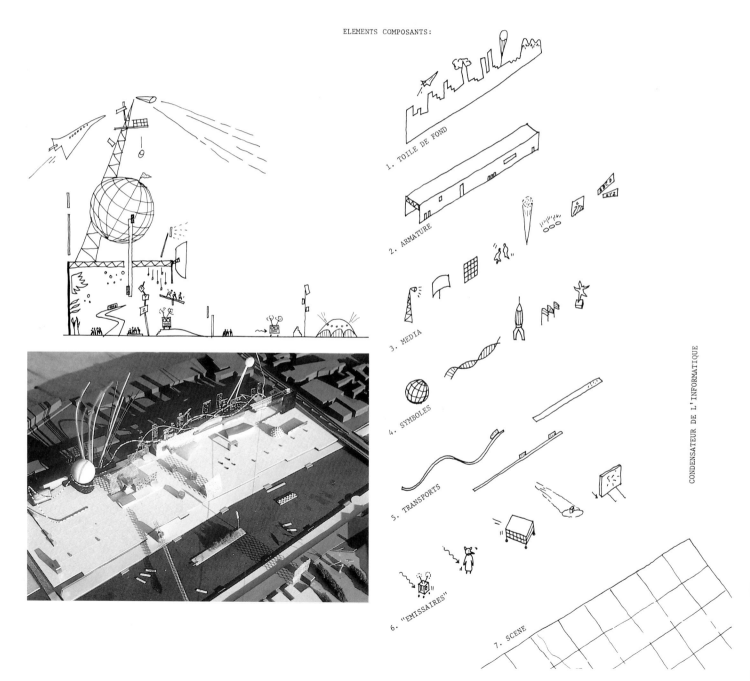

ELEMENTS COMPOSANTS:

1. TOILE DE FOND

2. ARMATURE

3. MEDIA

4. SYMBOLES

5. TRANSPORTS

6. "EMISSAIRES"

7. SCENE

CONDENSATEUR DE L'INFORMATIQUE

East site

Left

Diagram of points of interest along the Seine

Right

Diagram of water transportation, including

pleasure boats and public transport

Bottom

Overlay of circulation and movement diagrams

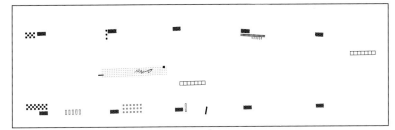

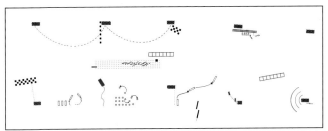

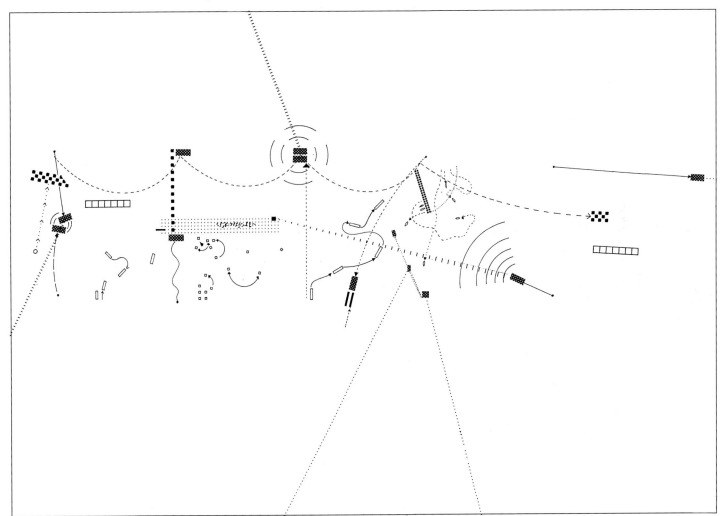

Bijlmermeer
Amsterdam-South 1986–1987

Our project for Bijlmermeer consists of a proposal for the renovation of the urban pattern of a rigid, resolutely modern complex of social housing situated to the southeast of Amsterdam. When we started the project apocalyptic visions were in the air; even those at the very highest administrative levels were envisioning the demolition of important sections of the complex.

We looked at it in a positive manner, especially the importance of its scale and the repetition of the compositional elements. At the same time we considered this monotonous beauty the very basis of a problem: as on the scale of a provincial town, urban living would henceforth be reduced to such completely innocent activities as fishing, walking, and bathing.

Bijlmermeer is generally considered the central area of this part of Amsterdam, constructed following the example of the Modern movement: eleven-storey slabs straddling two-storey pedestals, placed at equal intervals within a hexagonal grid; a uniform model disposed on an undifferentiated landscape, divided by a system of elevated, two-level roadways; parking garages parallel to the highways that act as buffers between the housing and the roads, while at the same time leaving the ground free. This system houses, albeit in a glaucous atmosphere, the secondary social, commercial, and cultural centers.

The all-pervasive buildings of the complex are the focus of its criticism, yet they are the least easily changed part. In our opinion it is not so much the buildings that determine the urban quality; rather, here it is more at ground level, in the open space between buildings, where ambitions, qualities, and impossibilities should be developed.

To prove this quality we projected a significant part of Bijmermeer onto other fragments of the urban fabric.

A mere quarter of the slabs nearly covered the entire center of Amsterdam—showing the ability of such a structure to suggest an interesting system of buildings.

Conclusion: the range of activities currently offered at Bijlmermeer and their urban quality are insufficient. The area is not compatible with our culture of congestion and seems anachronistic in light of the pluralism of modern urban life.

For us, Bijlmermeer is a solid, even monumental complex—the diagrams showing the existing buildings only serve to further this view. The secondary commercial centers require as much attention as the primary one, which is currently thriving owing to its proximity to the railroad and metro station to the west. However, the pedestrian paths leading to these secondary centers must be dissociated from the elevated roadways (which now act as overhead canopies).

Given its central location in the western conurbation of Holland and its good rail and road connections, Bijlmermeer can potentially become a self-contained urban entity. But Bijlmermeer must not be seen from the point of view of historic models— the possibilities of modern architecture are not yet exhausted. Unique in its class, this urbanistic model asks of architecture the difficult task of original creation.

Two Projects

The project was implemented in two phases. The first defined and developed a part of the project; the second tested the potentialities of the hypothesis generated in the first phase, using different areas of Bijlmermeer.

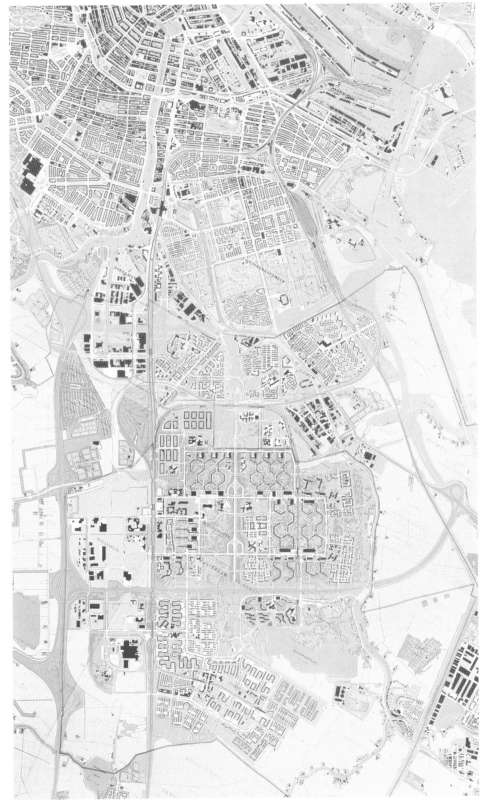

First project

The secondary commercial centers linked to the elevated roadways were demolished and reconstructed on paved squares, transforming the roadways from oppressive ceilings into veritable cement canopies. The parking garages were also demolished; in their place were built ramps allowing direct access to parking areas at ground level. These ramps, with entrances close to the apartment buildings, integrate a variety of programs.

The diversity of concentrations allows for a differentiation of green spaces; trees, shrubs, and ponds were grouped in a dense park, freeing space for lawns and solitary trees. The subway line to the east structures an axis grouping important sports facilities including a pool and a soccer stadium. The housing complex itself is enriched with several new typologies, in addition to the existing townhouses, villas with patios, and apartments redistributed among the existing slabs. The first floor acquires transparence as the surrounding green spaces are densified and the lower levels of the slabs are opened up.

Second project

The park is constructed with bands alternately containing villas and townhouses. The very notion of "park" is anachronistic, given the scale of the green space between the slabs. Office towers and high-technology workshops are projected for the north-south oriented band; the east-west band—the Bijlmer Strip—contains a variety of functions: in the north, economic activities; in the south, cultural and educational functions; west of the railroad tracks, a park for a variety of activities. The network of roads is doubled by a structural grid linking the principal points of interest.

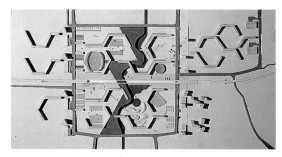

Below right

Site plan of the first project

Below left

Plan of the existing buildings projected
onto part of the historic fabric of Amsterdam

Right

View of the model

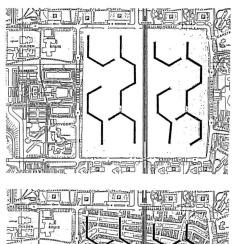

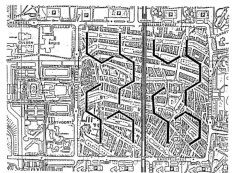

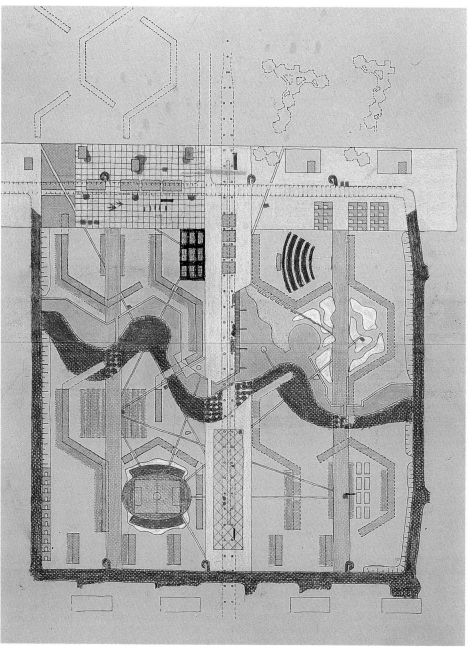

Sketches for the reurbanization of
the central axis (first project)

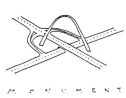

M O N U M E N T

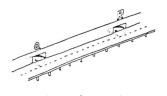

C A R - R A M P S

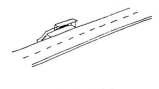

B U S H A L T E

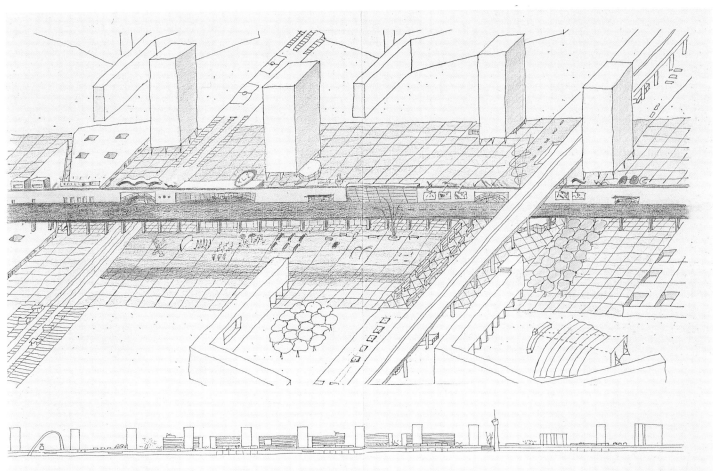

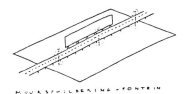

M U U R S C H I L D E R I N G - F O N T E I N

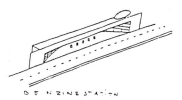

B E N Z I N E S T A T I O N

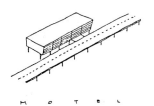

M O T E L

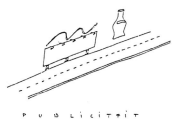

P U B L I C I T E I T

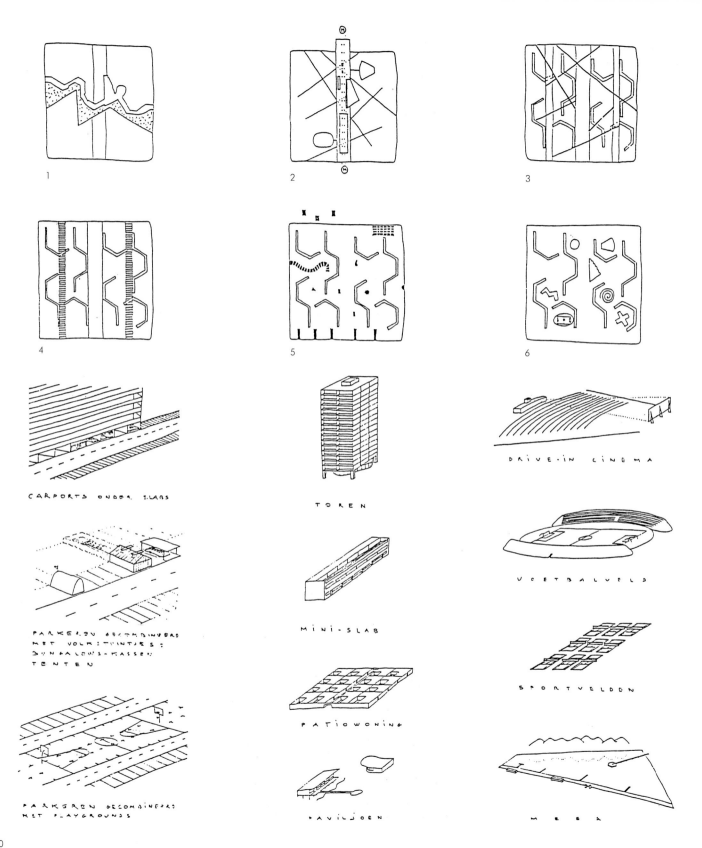

1

2

3

4

5

6

CARPORTS ONDER SLABS

TOREN

DRIVE-IN CINEMA

PARKEREN GECOMBINEERD MET VOLKSTUINTJES: BUNGALOWS-KASSEN TENTEN

MINI-SLAB

VOETBALVELD

PARKEREN GECOMBINEERD MET PLAYGROUNDS

PATIOWONING

SPORTVELDEN

PAVILJOEN

WEG

Facing page

The various programmatic elements:

1. The park, 2. The viaduct, 3. Circulation,

4. Parking, 5. New building typologies,

6. Sports and leisure facilities

Below

The existing fabric:

The buildings within the project, the

system of roads, plans superimposed

and elaborated using computer

graphics (second project)

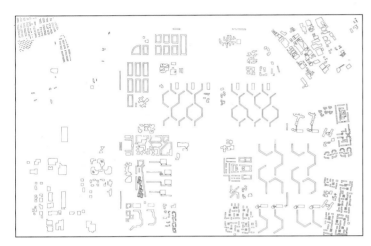

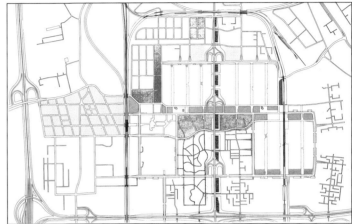

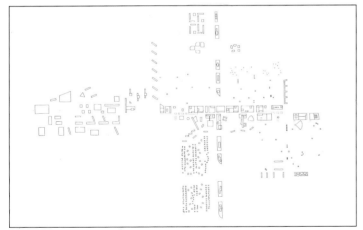

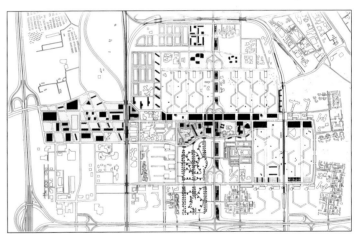

Top to bottom

Study diagram

Site plan showing the area of intervention

Perspective drawing along the principal axis

(second project)

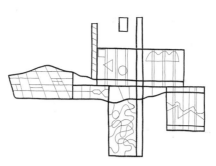

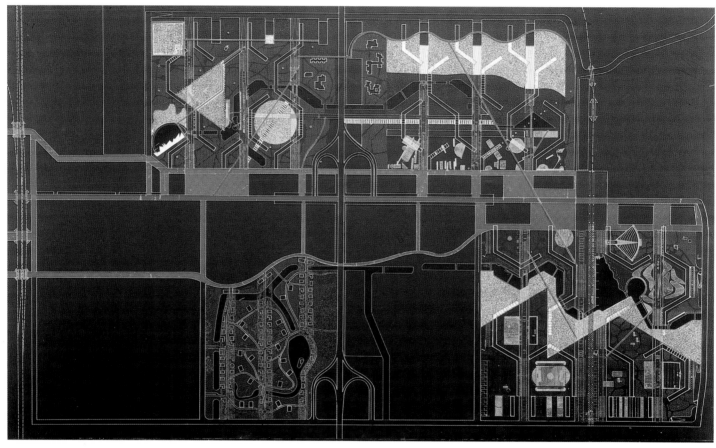

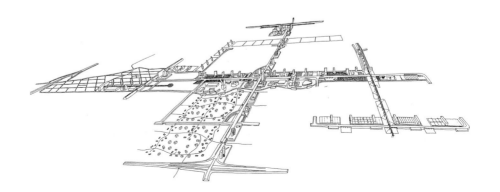

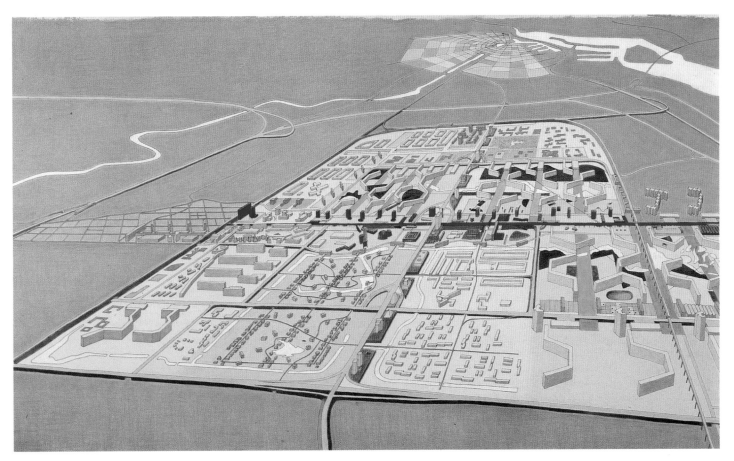

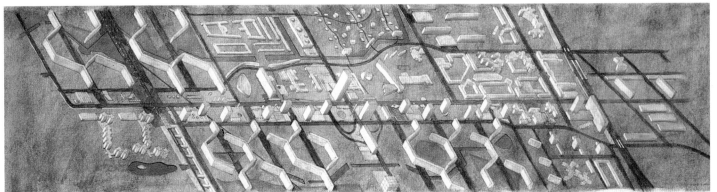

Urban Planning Competition
New Town of Melun-Sénart 1987

Left
Diagram of the project superimposed
on a plan of Paris
Right
View of the model

The site of Melun-Sénart is too beautiful to imagine a new city there with innocence and impunity; the expanse of the countryside, the beauty of the forests, and the serenity of the farms are an overwhelming presence, potentially at odds with any process of development. It requires a second innocence to believe today that urban development can be reasonably predicted and controlled. Too many architects' "visions" have disappeaed in their "dreams" of new additions to this chimerical army.

While the built and the solid are now beyond control—subject to political, financial and cultural forces in a perpetual state of flux—the same is not true of the void, perhaps the last subject about which architectural certitudes are still convincing.

The Voids: Bands

The essence of this project is a system of voids—in bands—inscribed into the site like a Chinese ideogram. We propose to direct the development of Melun-Sénart towards protecting and maintaining these voids. Certain of these are, in part, pieces of the existing landscape, situated to bring together both the maximum amount of beauty and the most historical fragments. The bands following the path of the major streets create controlled urban elements, while others distribute the major components of the new town on the site. It is our thesis that if this system of bands is established, the town of Melun-Sénart will be guaranteed beauty, serenity, accessibility, and urban services, regardless of the architecture that is to come.

The Islands: Interbands

In our proposal, the voids define an archipelago of residual islands—the interbands—differentiated in their sizes, shapes, locations, and confrontations with the various bands. Each island can be developed almost completely independently of the others; the archipelago model insures that the islands' unlimited freedom ultimately reinforces the coherence of the whole.

Each island will be designed with great care; our proposal does not imply that the islands can be neglected, but rather that the islands should be freely conceived as functions of their scale. Thus it is possible to concentrate on their contexts and on their interactions with the bands and with the town as a whole.

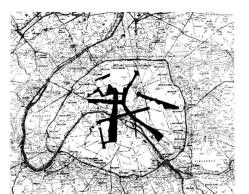

Above

Site plan with the various

functional bands

Below

Detail of the model

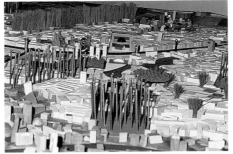

Diagrams with the elements of the project
and table showing the superposition of the
various bands: 1. Band of connections,
2. Circulation band, 3. Programmatic
band, 4. Landscaped band, 5. Band of
voids, 6.–7. Border bands

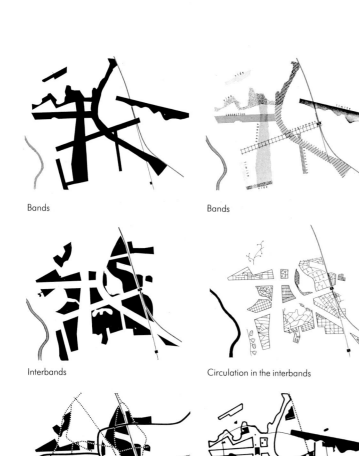

Bands

Bands

Interbands

Circulation in the interbands

Principal axes

Recreational facilities

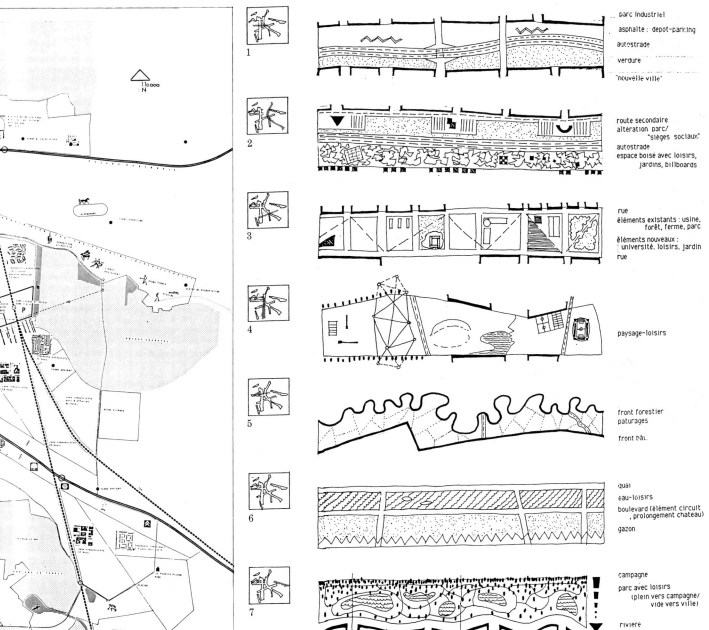

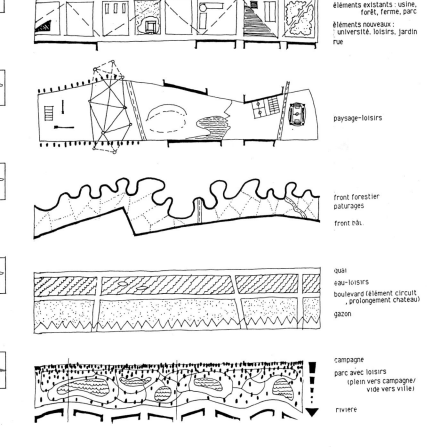

1   parc industriel

asphalte : depot-parking

autostrade

verdure

"nouvelle ville"

2   route secondaire

altération parc/
    "sièges sociaux"

autostrade

espace boisé avec loisirs,
    jardins, billboards

3   rue

éléments existants : usine,
    forêt, ferme, parc

éléments nouveaux :
    université, loisirs, jardin

rue

4   paysage-loisirs

5   front forestier

paturages

front bât.

6   quai

eau-loisirs

boulevard (élément circuit
    , prolongement chateau)

gazon

7   campagne

parc avec loisirs
    (plein vers campagne/
    vide vers ville)

riviere

International Business Center
Lille 1989

In Lille, on a site between the city and the suburbs, a new station for the TGV is planned. The site will be detached from a parcel of highway interchanges to make room for the International Business Center. From the point of view of the metropolis of Lille, the project for the international railway station constitutes a two-kilometer-long linear interface between the historic center and the suburbs. From the point of view of the north European "triangle," the new station, with its cross-Channel connections, will become the node between London, Paris, Brussels, the Ruhr, and Rotterdam. The TGV will unite these urban agglomerations, reshaping the psychological space of Europe. The project responds to a double ambition for the city: to plan the sector near the center which, since the time of Vauban, has been a gash in the city; and to realize a sophisticated urban reinforcement, a bridge-head to the North Region. The spatial and temporal relationships between the International Business Center and the Lille-Lesquin airport will be concurrent with those of Paris/Roissy or of London/Heathrow.

In our age dominated by (tele)communication technologies, the project links a tertiary center, a meeting and conference center, a scientific park, a park for expositions and fairs, theaters, cinemas, a shopping mall, galleries, recreational facilities, housing for staff and students, and a ten-hectare urban park. The project is also served by a advanced system of transportation: two metro lines, a tramway, parking lots, the subterranean peripheral boulevard, the TGV station, and an important regional station.

The geometries of built form in eastern Lille necessitate an underground route for the TGV, which risks rendering invisible this key element of the complex. The project calls attention to the TGV with a triangular plaza in front of the station, bordered by a shopping mall and a ramp leading to the park. On the east side of the station is a Piranesian space which assures in spectacular fashion a vertical connection between all the transportation methods on the site.

The "triangle of stations" facilitates connections between the new TGV and the existing regional stations. The TGV station comprises a superstructure of high-rise office buildings situated above public galleries. To the east, parallel to the TGV station and over the parking lots and covered boulevard, is a series of smaller office buildings, situated in a garden. Further east are apartment buildings, assuring a transition to the traditional quarter. South of the stations are public administration buildings, exhibition halls, and the conference center—a bridge spanning the river of railroad tracks.

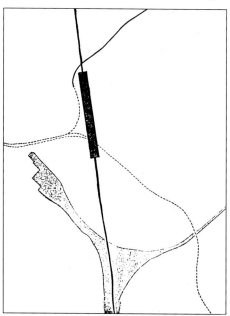

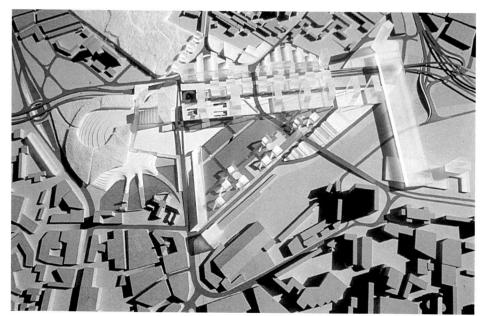

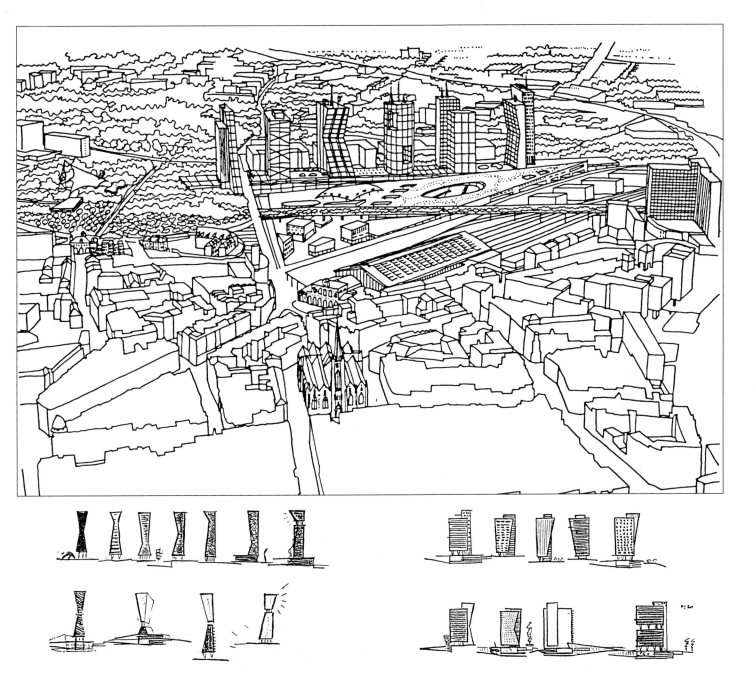

Below, top to bottom
Sketches for train station,
parking garage, and
infrastructural node

Study sketch

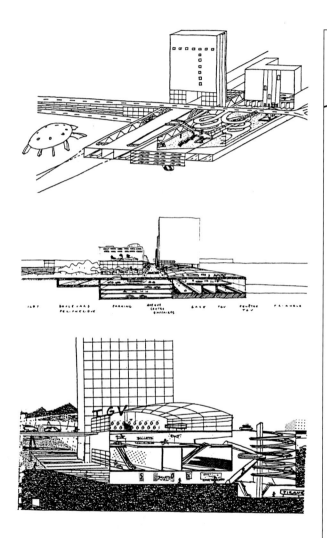

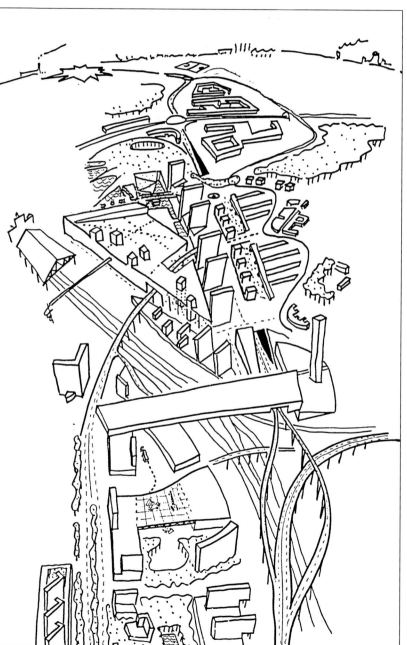

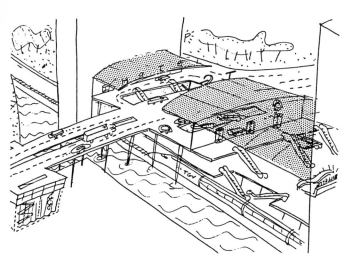

Intersection of rue Le Corbusier with the east-west axis of the TGV station

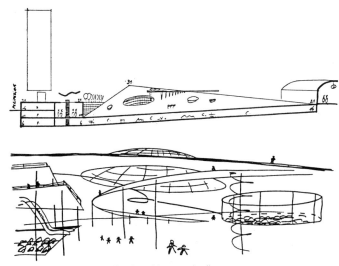

Triangle connecting the principal levels and the central gallery

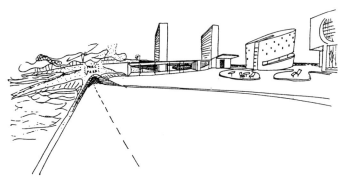

Perspective toward the convention center

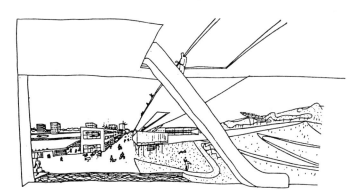

Perspective of the train station toward the city

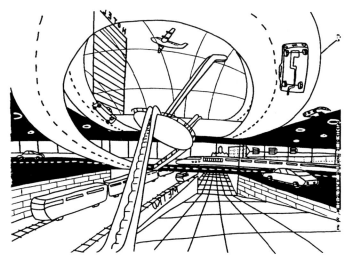

Network of communication lines

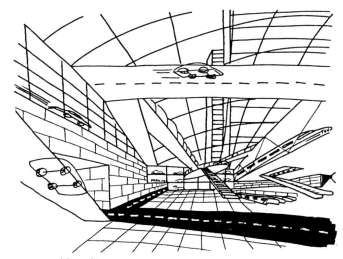

Perspective toward the parking garage

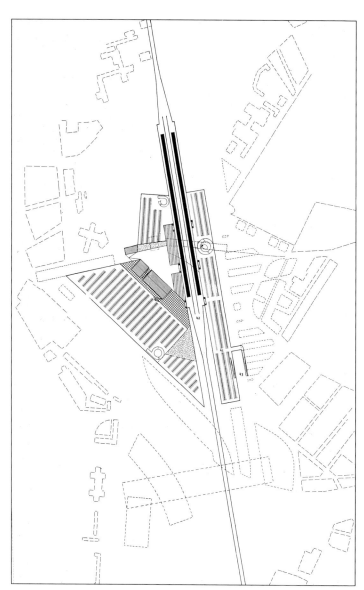

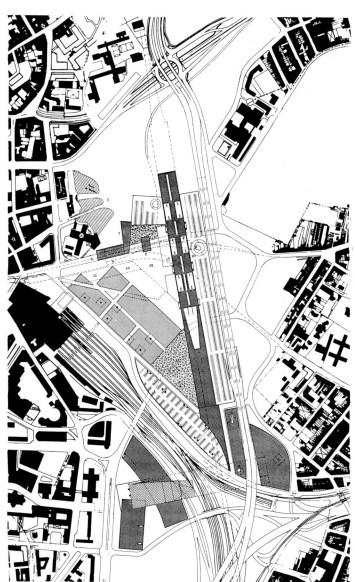

Level +14m Platforms and plazas of the TGV station

Level +21m Gallery of the TGV station

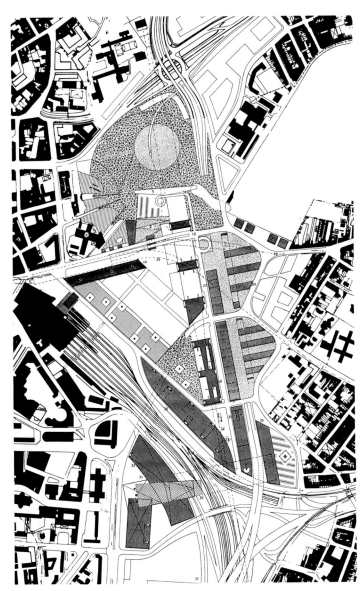

Level +25.5m Business gallery

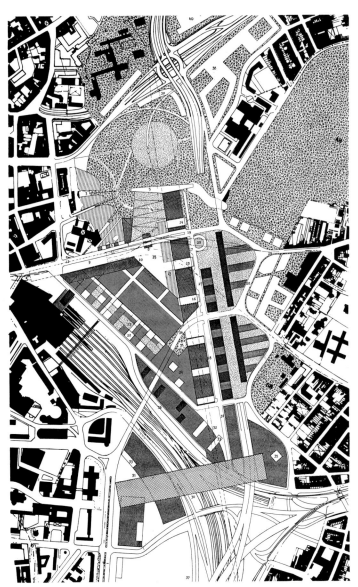

Site plan

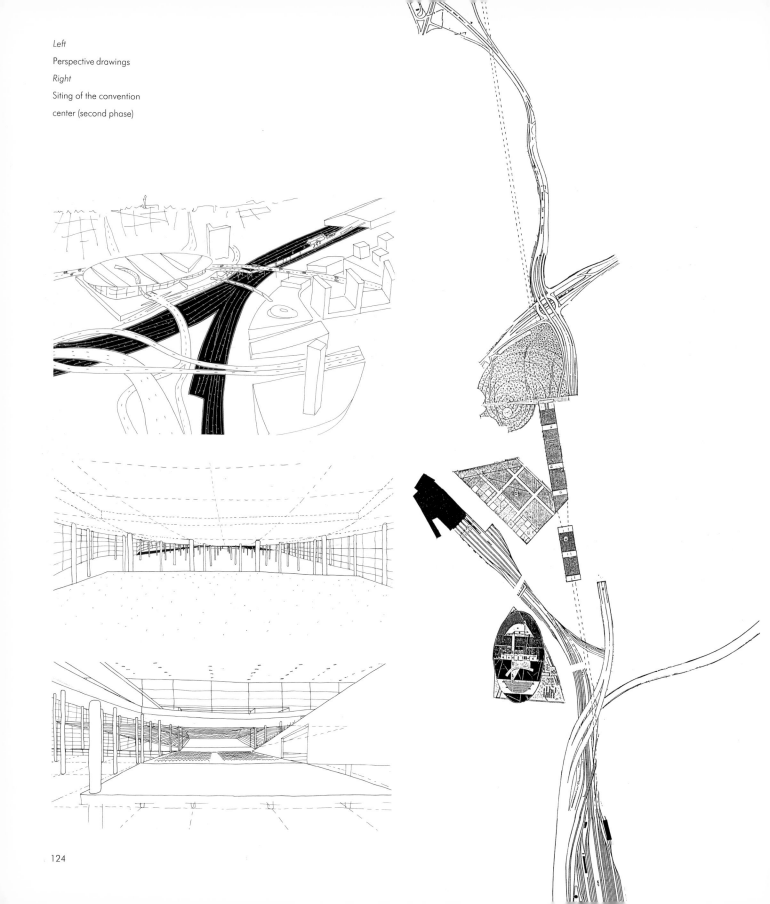

Left

Perspective drawings

Right

Siting of the convention

center (second phase)

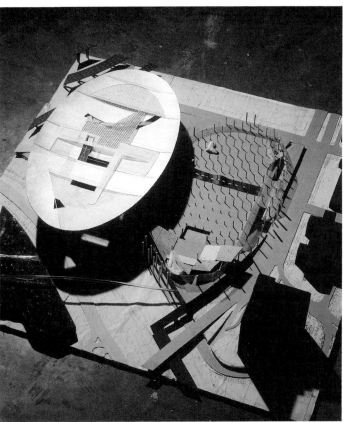

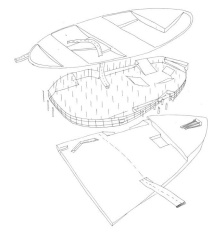

Sections and plan studies showing the
differentiation of the various interior elements
of the convention center (second phase)

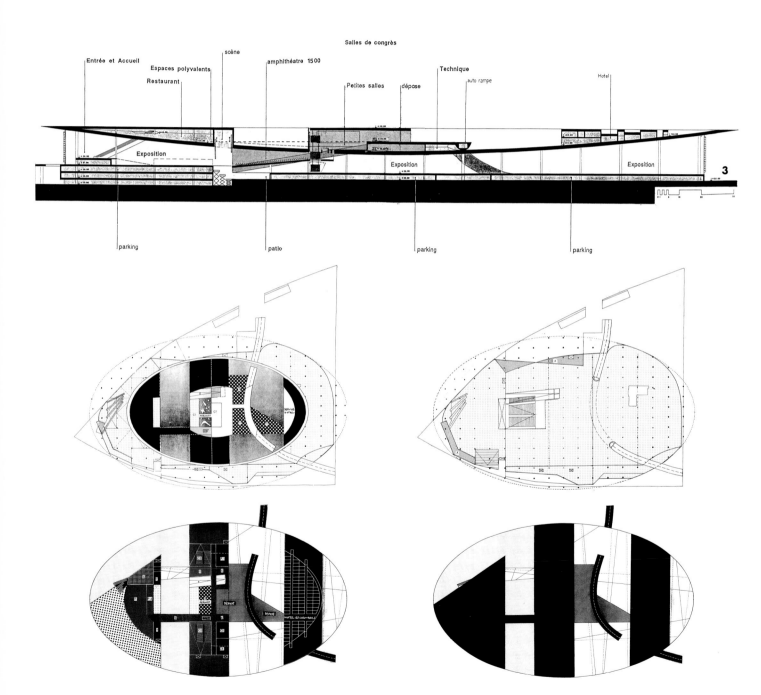

Vertical Projects

Sea Trade Center
Zeebrugge 1989

To offer an alternative to the tunnel under the English Channel, the ferry companies between Great Britain and the Continent seek to imagine more exciting crossings. Our project opts for a form which shrinks from the recognizable and prefers instead to evoke successive associations: mechanical, industrial, utilitarian, abstract, poetic, surrealist. The project attempts to be at the same time fully artistic and totally efficient. The chosen theme is "a Tower of Babel without fault," dedicated to the new ambition of Europe and the function of the terminal: the cosmopolitan *mélange* of visitors. Differing from the "original" Tower of Babel, which was a symbol of ambition, of chaos, and finally of powerlessness, the present Tower of

Babel is a functional "machine" which painlessly welcomes travellers, sorting them out and placing them on their proper paths, according to their destinations.

The building itself is a cross between a sphere and a cone. The two lower levels direct traffic to and from the building. We sought maximum efficiency: even in the case of the simultaneous boarding and disembarkation of four boats, the configuration of land-bound traffic and the separations within the building allow different activities to occur without interference.

A bus circulation level tops this sorting operation. For the passengers' comfort this is directed by a separate loop outside the building. Overhead snake two levels of parking

in an ascending spiral. This spiral culminates in a great public hall offering a panoramic view onto the sea and the countryside. Higher up, the cone divides into vertical segments: a distinct office tower inside the spherical form, a half-moon for the hotel, and a segment for administrative services. The space between these parts reveals a view of the sky, while the glass floor allows the gaze to fall down below. "Roofed" under the cupola, these parts are connected by aerial passageways. The terrace on top of the hotel is set up like the former casinos on the North Sea. The amphitheater, which looks out onto the basin, is atop the administrative and promotional complex, and also serves as a conference center.

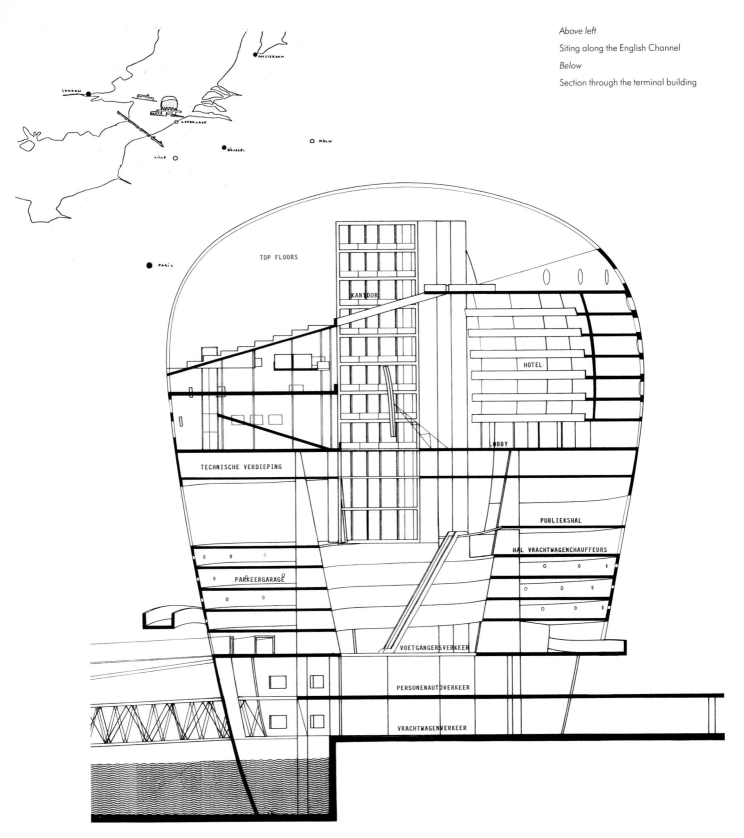

TOP FLOORS

KANTOOR

HOTEL

LOBBY

TECHNISCHE VERDIEPING

PUBLIEKSHAL

HAL VRACHTWAGENCHAUFFEURS

PARKEERGARAGE

VOETGANGERSVERKEER

PERSONENAUTOVERKEER

VRACHTWAGENVERKEER

Below

Studies of the interior: perspectives and sections

Right

Plans of various levels

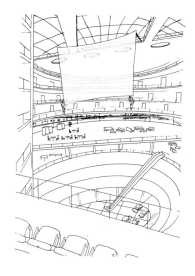

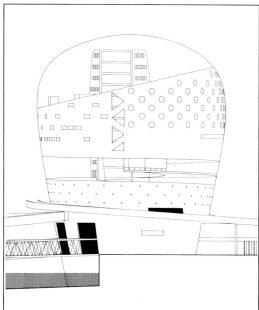

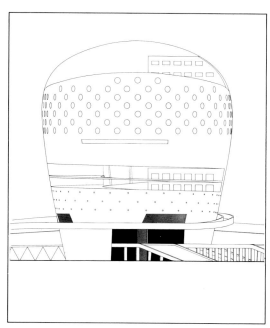

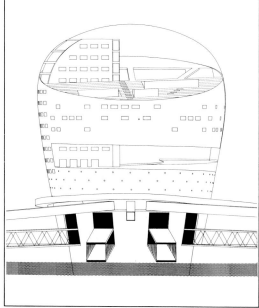

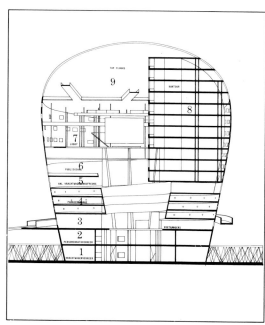

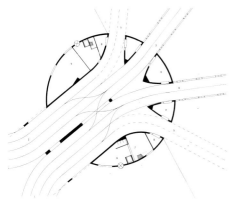

1. Vehicular access

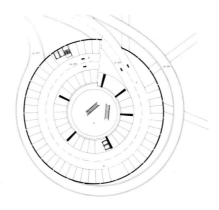

4. Parking garage

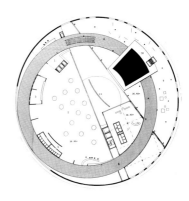

7. Hall

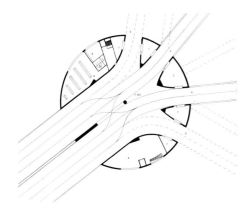

2. Vehicular access

5. Truckers' level

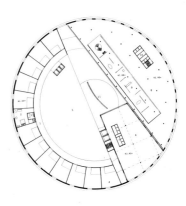

8. Hotel and offices

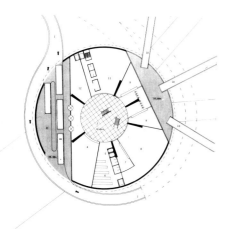

3. Pedestrian access

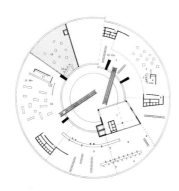

6. Travelers' level

9. Terraces

National Library of France
Paris 1989

Views of the model

Intent

At a time when the electronic revolution seems to be dissolving everything solid, imagining the ultimate library seems tenuous at best. The purpose of this project is to divest architecture of duties it can no longer fulfill, and to explore aggressively its new freedom. The project is based on technological scenarios worked out with inventors and systems analysts from electronics corporations who have assured us that the utopian integration of all the information systems will be realized before the building opens. These systems permit the simultaneous reading of books, films, music, and computers in the form of electronic "magic tablets." Therefore, this is not the end of "the book," but a period of new equality. But most of all, these scenarios are exciting in that they give notice that, faced with electronic automation, the latest function of architecture will be to create symbolic spaces that respond to the persistent desire for collectivity.

Concept

The library is interpreted as a solid block of information, a storehouse for all forms of memory: books, laserdiscs, microfiches, computers. In this block, public spaces are defined as *absences of the built*, voids dug out of the mass of information. These absences are presented as multiple embryos floating in the stacks—each one endowed with a technological placenta of its own. Defined as holes, the spatialities of the individual libraries can be explored according to their inherent logic, independently from one another, the exterior envelope and the usual constraints of architecture, including the laws of gravity. Together, they imply a spectrum of spatial experiences that runs from

the conventional to the experimental. The revolutionary potential of the elevator has always been to introduce—by its capacity to establish mechanical rather than architectural relationships—a new era of liberated and problematic relationships between diverse components of a building. This is why the connection between the principal interior spaces of the library is a group of nine elevators which cross the block at regular intervals.

Planning

We dismissed our original project—a horizontal building—for two reasons: first, in an area dominated by two megaliths (the new Ministry of Finance and the Omnisport Palace at Bercy), any low building placed in this landscape devoid of scale would seem subjugated to them and have no impact on the expressway, the river, or the park; and second, the importance given to the frequency and explosive interactions of the programmatic elements across the site presupposes a nightmarish density of circulation.
In its proposed position, the building proclaims a new intent for the neighborhood of Tolbiac:
1. It reinforces the idea of moving the RER (Regional Express Rail) station.
2. In place of the two collections of buildings serving as bookends on either side of the library, these complementary structures could be regrouped in order to define a continuation of rue Clisson.
3. The existing footbridge—here made of still-living timbers that change color according to the seasons—serves not only a cultural destination but feeds into a new center.
4. The siting of the principal volume creates a zigzag across the Seine between the library, the new Ministry of Finance, the

Arab Institute, Notre Dame, and so on.

Siting

The library is positioned in the eastern part of the site. The conference center runs along rue Tolbiac and benefits from a distinguished entrance that opens onto the Seine. Between the center and the library, a forum embraces all the preliminary elements of the program—spaces for welcoming guests, information, and exhibition—arranged to be open and flexible, organized more in terms of defined units. The forum extends to the bank of the Seine in order to absorb pedestrian flow.

Along the new avenue, a system of ramps allows the public access to the forum and to the different parking levels—the parking opens onto the axis of rue Domrémy, providing a special privilege to visitors from the thirteenth *arrondissement*. These ramps create several distinct entrances leading to offices, services, delivery areas, and technical spaces, grouped in a service block running parallel to the railroad track. West of the library, an open-air version of the forum is planned. A forest of Lebanese Cedars forms a vault shadowing a little park. A wall of water flows out of the forum, losing itself in the forest, thus creating, across from the building, an open-air patio/café which, on special occasions, can be transformed into a court of honor. Along the Seine, a tunnel leads directly to the parking garages.

The Library

The *Great Ascending Hall* precisely emphasizes the building's organization, where the entire block seems to be carried by the transparent shafts of the nine elevators. The ceiling is made of glass, displaying the "treasures" of the building above the visitors' heads. On the walls of the elevator shafts, a vertical illuminated directory shows the different destinations—fragments of texts, titles, names, songs, and so on. This perpetual ascending motion creates the illusion that the whole building rests on the signs of an eternal countdown to lift-off. Each elevator leads to a different destination; while climbing in their glass tubes to their respective destinations, the elevators traverse the other libraries with a discrete hush. Toward the bottom, the Great Ascending Hall issues onto:

1. The pebbles: *the Library of Image and Sound*
The rooms and booths reserved for films, television programs, and music are set into the podium and connected to each other with a ramp. Near the top, the Great Ascending Hall meets the intersection in a sequence reflecting its anticipated popularity.

2. The intersection: *the Library of Current Events*
Two voids intersect each other: the horizontal lecture room and audio-visual spaces; and a continuous auditorium which descends towards the river. At the intersection: an ampitheater. In the walls: video booths.

3. The spiral: *the Study Library*
It is composed of a continuous spiral which, in three helixes, connects five levels of open stacks, carrels, and study booths. The intersections with the different levels allow for thematic and spatial variations.

4. The shell: *the Catalog Room*
From the outside this resembles a small gem, connecting the *spiral* to the *buckle* and looking out onto Paris.

5. The buckle: *the Research Library*
This has a scientific interior where the ground floor transforms itself into partitions, which change into a ceiling, which breaks again into partitions; a Möbius strip closes the buckle in the building's catacombs.

6. The summit: a restaurant, a gymnasium, a garden and a swimming pool.
Though each library has its own elevator, the block is also perforated with escalators which snake from the ground floor to the roof. All other floors hold various installations of stacks. The north side of the building houses administrative services and personnel offices which can be directly connected to the stacks or to the principal halls.

The Facades

The glass facades offer varying degrees of transparency. The materials are partially silk-screened to give the impression of passing clouds. The lighting reveals, on the interior of the building, its fathomable (and unfathomable) depths. Other elements—the catalog room, the intersections—have windows and thus appear as polished gems or tunnels in a nebulous mass.

Technical features

The structure and the concept of the services reinforces the division of the building between the stacks and the public. The zones allocated for various types of storage are defined by a series of parallel walls which also permit the division of the public open spaces. The walls, openings, and cavities are designed to allow easy installation and removal of cables in all parts of the building. Maintenance is therefore simplified due to the absence of conduits.

The public spaces each have their own mechanical rooms, situated to best fill the intervals between the cube and the interior spaces.

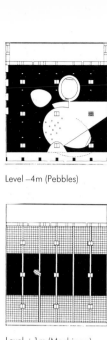

Level −4m (Pebbles)

Level −3m

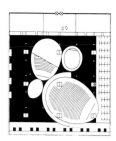

Level −2m

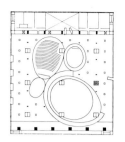

Level −1m

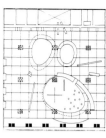

Level 0m (Ascending Hall)

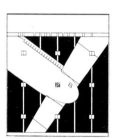

Level +1m (Machinery)

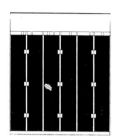

Level +2m (Stacks)

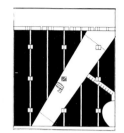

Level +3m (Intersection)

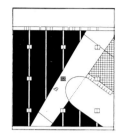

Level +4m

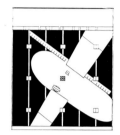

Level +5m

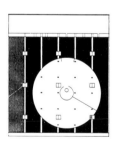

Level +6m

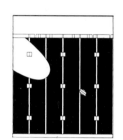

Level +7m

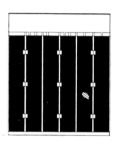

Level +8m

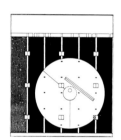

Level +9m

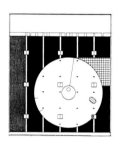

Level +10m

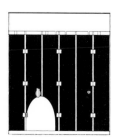

Level +11m

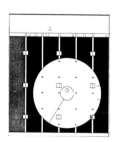

Level +12m

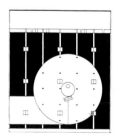

Level +13m

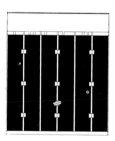

Level +14m

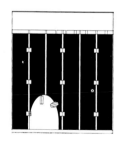

Level +15m (Shell)

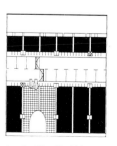

Level +16m

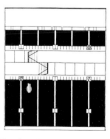

Level +17m (Buckle)

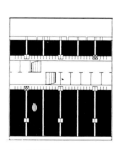

Level +18m

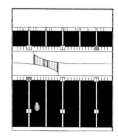

Level +19m

Level +20m

View of the model, axonometric, and site plan

Facing page

Plans of the various levels

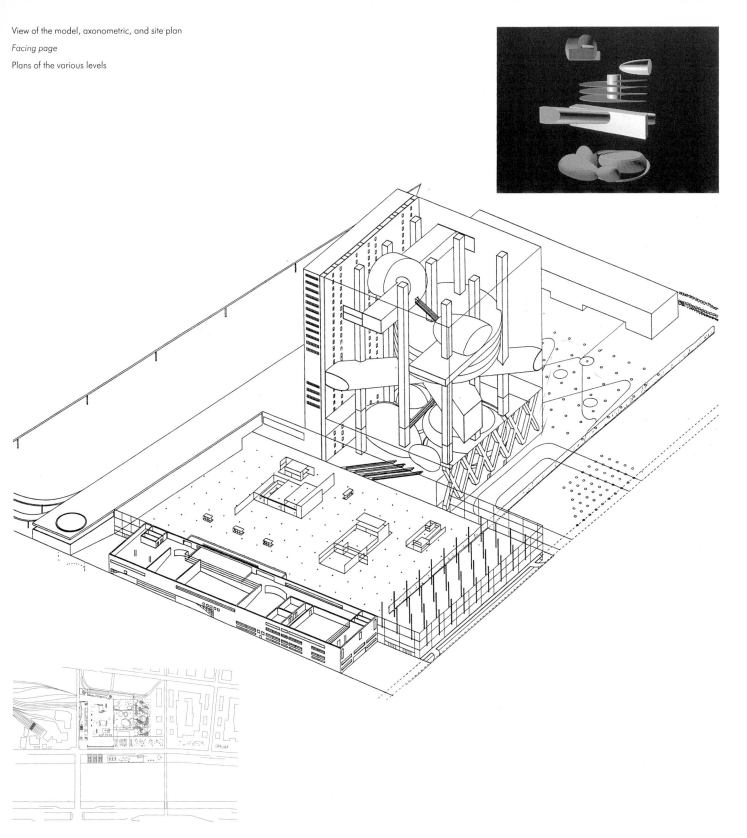

Schematic diagrams with various functions:

1. Stacks, 2. Library of Image and Sound,

3. Great Ascending Hall,

4. Library of Current Events,

5. Study Library, 6. Research Library,

7. Superposition of public spaces,

8. Wall structure and elevator grid

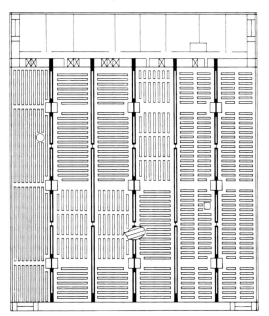

1. Stacks

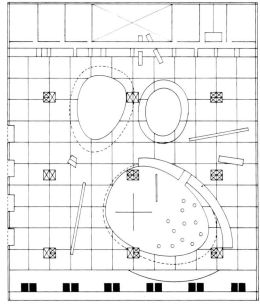

3. The Great Ascending Hall

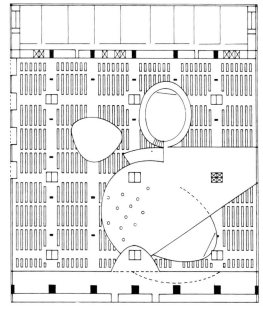

2. The Pebbles

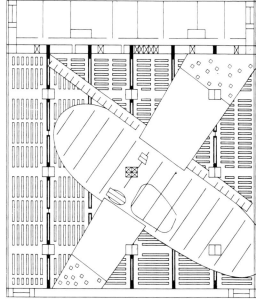

4. The Intersection

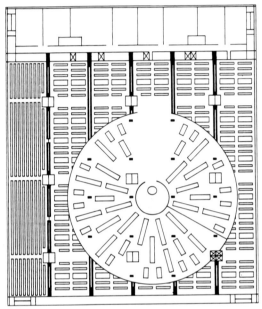

5. The Spiral

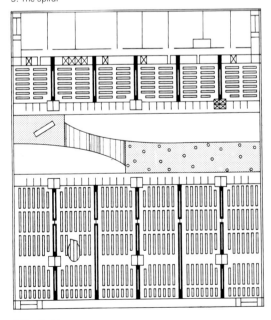

6. The Buckle

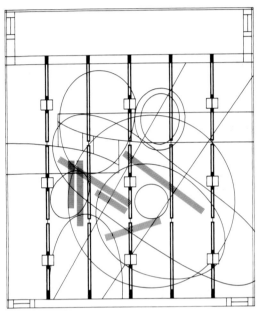

7. Superposition of public spaces

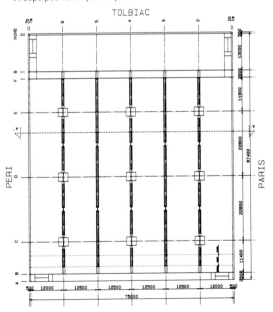

8. Diagram of wall structure

137

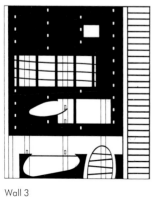

Wall 3

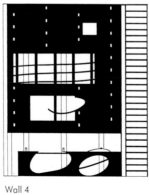

Wall 4

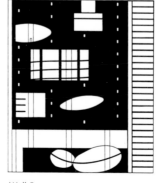

Wall 5

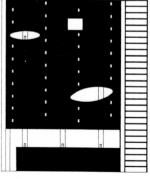

Wall 6

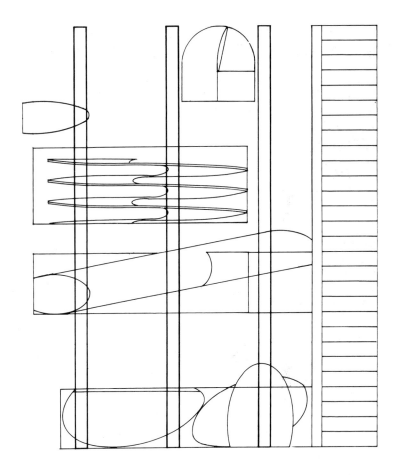

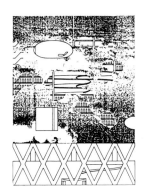

Facade overlooking the Seine

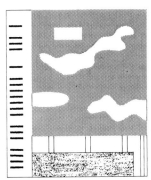

Facade toward the suburbs

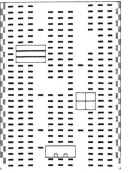

Facade toward rue de Tolbiac

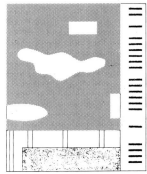

Facade toward Paris

Center for Art and Media Technology

Karlsruhe 1989

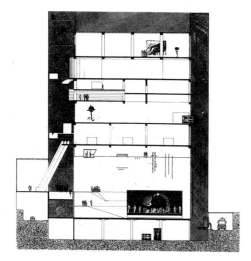

Theme

The siting and the program of the Center for Art and Media Technology (*Zentrum für Kunst und Medientechnologie*, ZKM) imply a series of relationships with the existing city that determine the project's general theme: 1) the *futurist* Center borders on the *classical* city of Karlsruhe; 2) the Center opens onto the *periphery*, although the train station is turned toward the *center city*; 3) part of the developed space is to be allocated for *artists*, the other for the *public*; 4) the Museum of Contemporary Art covers a musical-artistic field ranging from *traditional* exhibitions to *experimental* installations. Classical/futurist, center/periphery, public/artist, traditional/experimental: the aim of this project is to explore the fertile ground of these oppositions.

Concept

The premise of the competition was to avoid establishing a relationship with the train station. Any attempt at separation leaves only a narrow strip of land wedged between the street and the parking lot; building on this space implies an alignment with the railroad tracks.

Our project arises, however, from the opposite supposition: that maximum integration between station and Center increases the autonomy of both, while allowing them to interpenetrate. As if a third dimension were added to the two-dimensional plan of a Baroque city, the Center is constructed on a system of coordinates constituting the three axes x, y, and z. Each axis organizes one or more of the above-listed dichotomies.

X-axis: center-periphery

The x-axis determines the system of entrances. The passage under the railroad tracks is divided by a glass partition which penetrates into the main hall of the station, defining the entrance to the Center on the city side. This passage no longer exclusively leads to the platforms: the "artistic side", thus conceived, shelters the Media Technology Museum.

The visitors' obligatory north-south movement is reinforced by the chronological presentation of the history of media technology, culminating in the principal entrance with the "contemporary era."

The coexistence of two oppositions separated in this way--art and transport--sets the tone of the complex. The passage from historic to contemporary is conducted through a "time tunnel"; the inhabitants of the classical city are prepared for the new museum by their journey through the passage. At the southern extremity of the x-axis, a sloping plaza marks the entrance and connects to Schwarzwaldstraße, serving as a descending ramp for visitors to the museum. The space under this plaza is occupied by the theater foyer and the new hall for the ICE,[1] separated by a glass partition.

The x-axis facilitates the meeting of two different worlds at their extremities: on the city side, it becomes the Museum of the Station; on the south, the Station of the Museum.

Y-axis: artist-public

The y-axis represents the opposition between production and presentation.

The principal connecting element between the parking lot and the Center consists of a "museum platform" located at the same height (121m) as the future ICE tracks. It is separated from the station facilities by a transparent skin: for the first time, travellers and museum visitors are put face-to-face. At

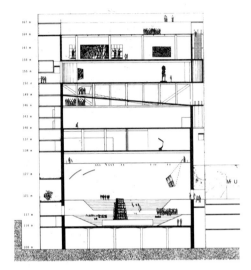

the point where the y-axis crosses the x-axis two separate entrances are found. East of the museum entrance the research departments are organized in parallel bands, perpendicular to the platform at the 121m level—an organization aiming to create a prominent "zone of confrontation" between the different intellectual territories. Underneath are spaces for professional research, organized in a group of studios on two levels (108m and 114m) situated between the multi-use space and the theater. The theater and studios are linked to the lower level by a great hallway at the 108m level, which also leads into the central studios. The roof (at 164m), contemporary equivalent of the railway station's plaza, can be used for open-air demonstrations and the presentation of scientific and artistic research conducted at the Center.

Z-axis: classical-futurist

The Museum of Contemporary Art is composed of a vertical sequence of several levels. It begins with a space equipped with leading-edge technology—the theater—and ends with a classic musical-artistic space, naturally lit; *a machine becomes a building.* Owing to the choice of a load-bearing metal structure, the floors requiring structural elements alternate with those levels not requiring any load support. The lower, square spaces of the museum (134m and 140m), do not receive any natural light. A sloping balcony, leading from the level at 134m to that at 140m, offers a view of the the city and accesses the conference halls and seminar rooms (146m to 149m). The second, circular space of the museum (152m), can be lit naturally or artificially. The non-load-bearing walls can eventually

be adapted for different configurations. The "interior building" is surrounded by four empty bands. On the south side is the "robot," an interpretation of the traditional scenery cage. It houses various technical equipment and movable elements permitting the composition of an "electronic decor" for each space. The fringes of the museum are thus available for numerous future potential uses. This visual spectacle can be seen from the highway on a translucent billboard—a veritable advertisement for the activities at the Center. On the city side, towards the north, rises an autonomous unit—comprising a network of elevators, ramps, escalators, and balconies—which only penetrates the core at the level of the conference hall. This network of circulation surrounding an enigmatic block of ever-changing artistic spaces creates tension and mystery. In proportion to the upwards movement, the view of the city becomes more and more impressive. The journey culminates in an open-air space and restaurant (at 164m). The break with the periphery and the *mise-en-scène* of the center city justifies the height of the museum.

So the visitor will always be able to understand the relationship between the spaces and their uses, the choice of verticality contributes, more than any form of horizontal organization, to the legibility of the different spaces and their different uses. The band located on the side of the entrance plaza is used for certain specific circulation functions; it can also serve the exterior balconies of several halls of the museum. On the west side of the building a row of services is projected, comprising housing, technical spaces, and other functional ties to the Center.

Right

Siting of the project

Below

East-west section

Bottom

First floor plan of professional

research space (first project)

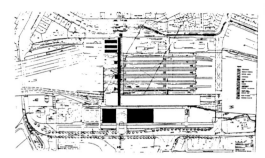

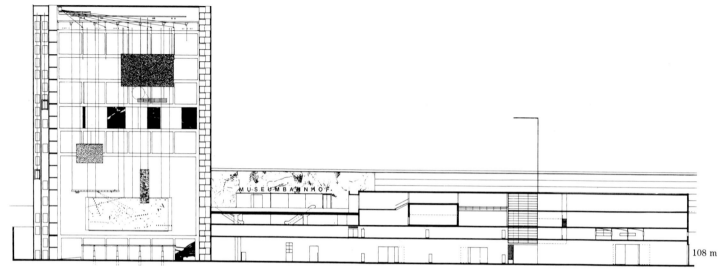

108 m

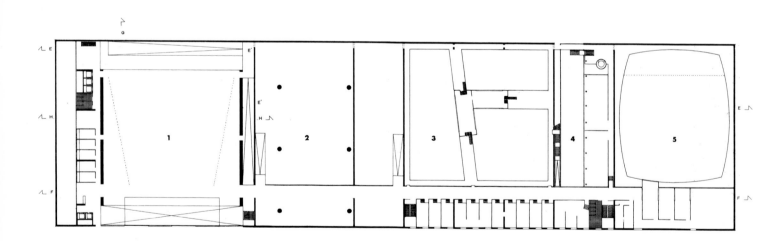

1. Theater

2. Technical and storage rooms

3. Open space above the grand studios

4. Ateliers

5. Open space above the multi-use room

Right

Study sketch

Below

Interior elevations

Bottom

Exterior elevations (first project)

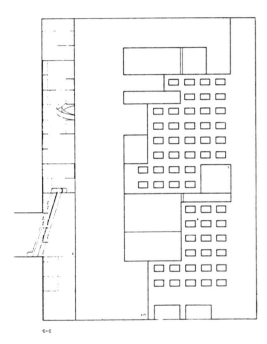

C-C

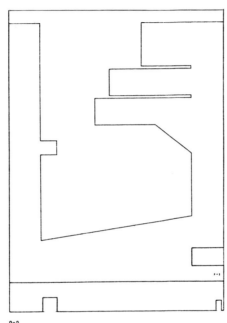

G-G

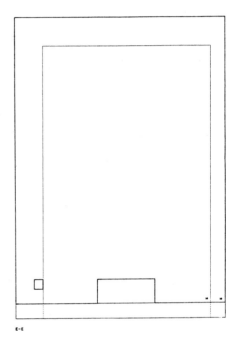

E-E

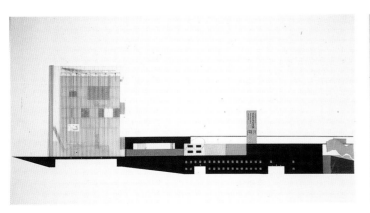

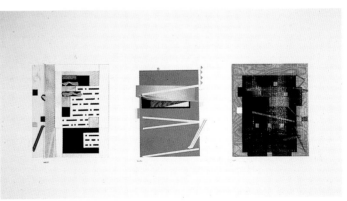

Elevation, view of model, and

section (second project)

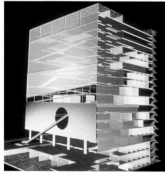

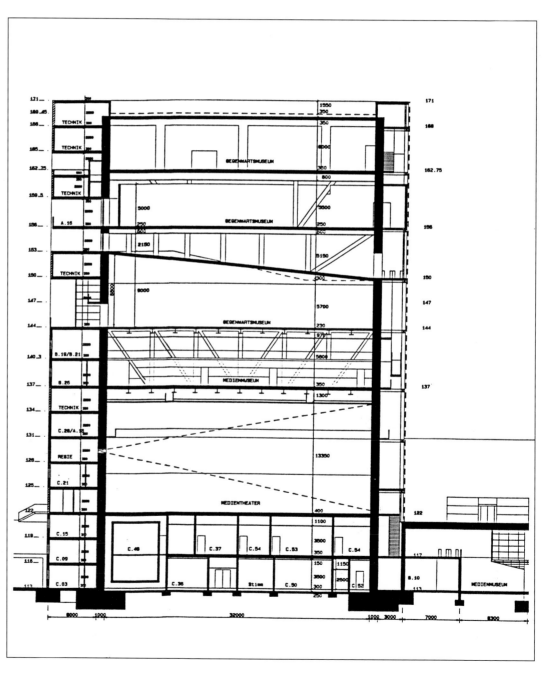

Siting of second project, plans,
and detail of the model

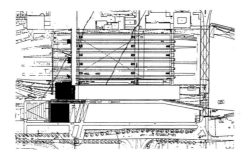

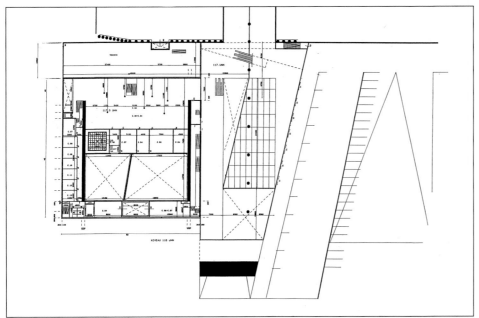

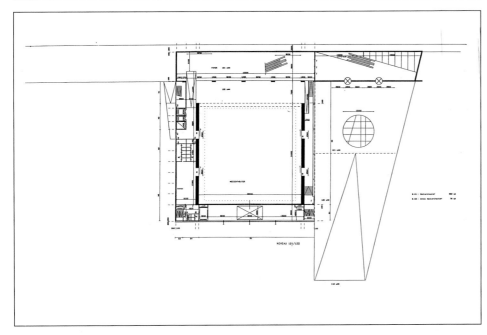

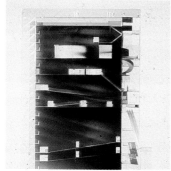

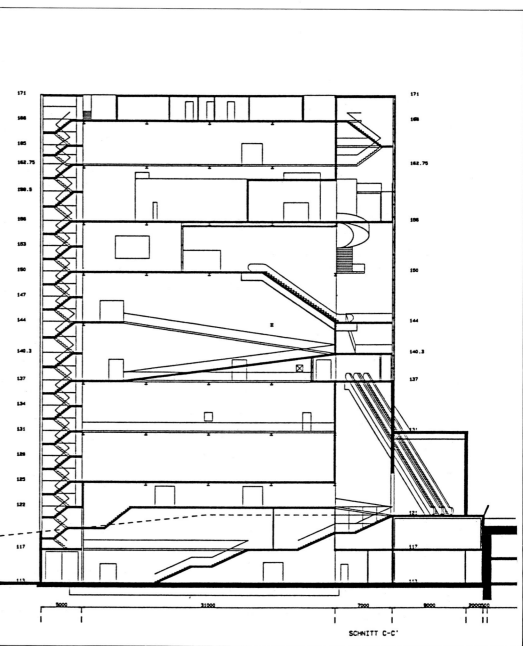

SCHNITT C-C'

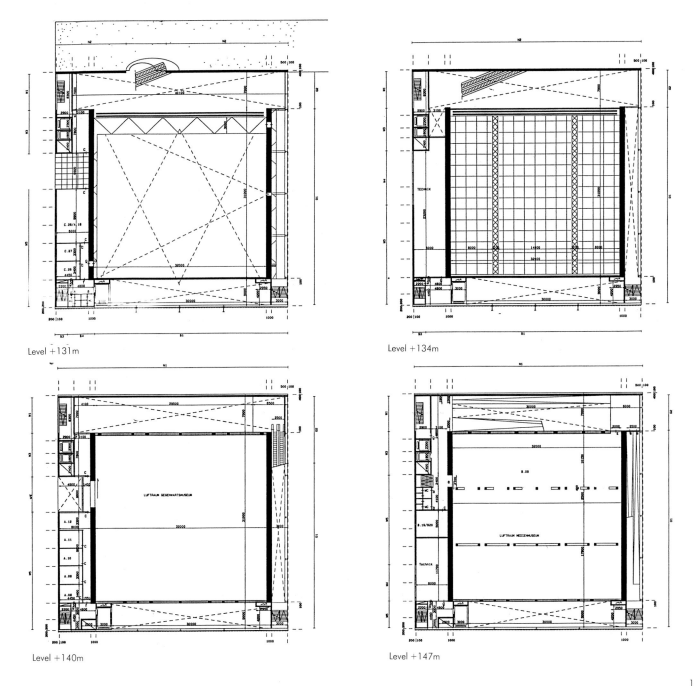

Level +131m

Level +134m

Level +140m

Level +147m

Diagram, details of the model,
and section (second project)

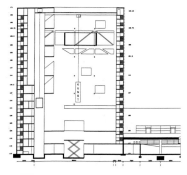

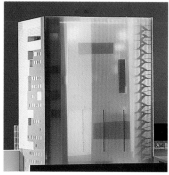

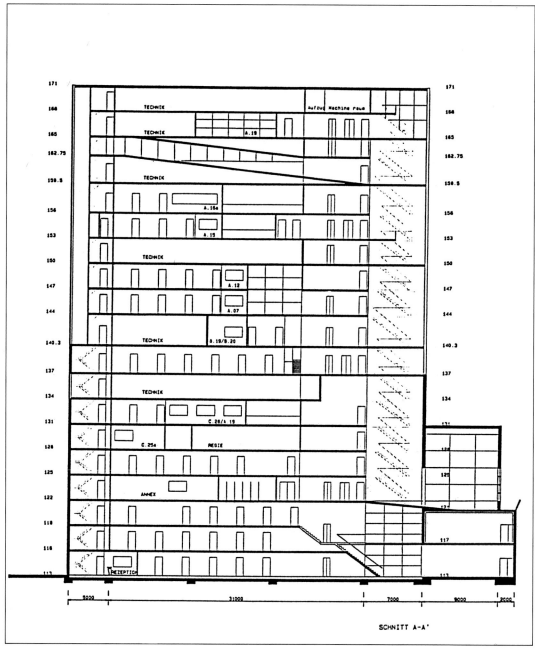

SCHNITT A-A'

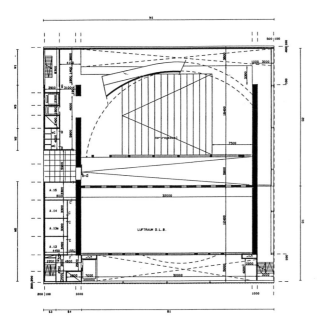

Level +153m

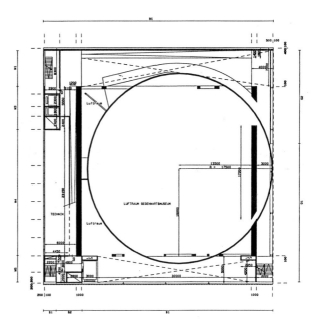

Level +159m

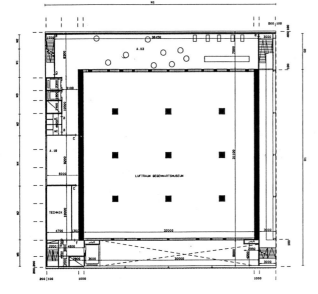

Level +165m

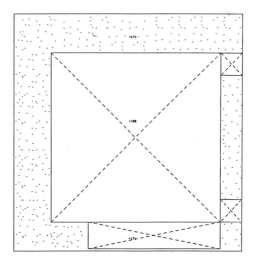

Level +171m

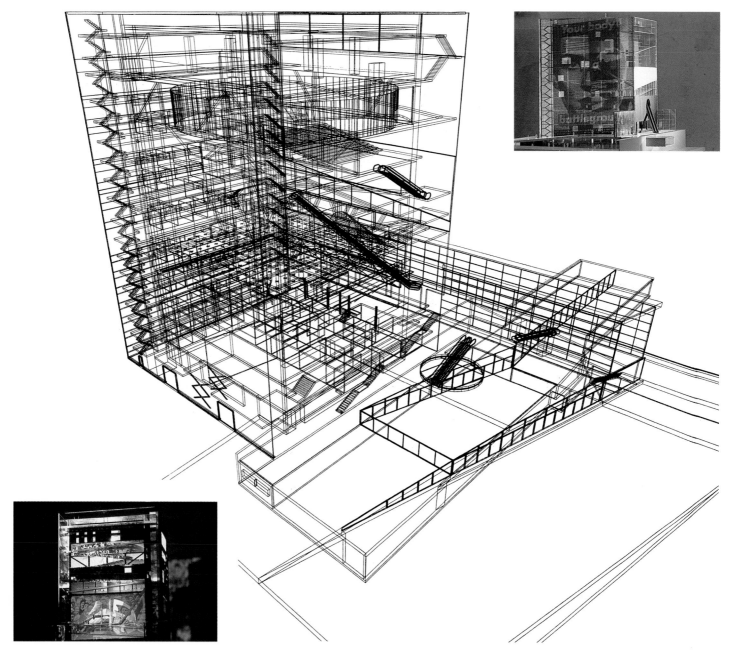

Architectural Writings

Project for the renovation of the
prison at Arnheim, 1978–1988

The New Sobriety
1981

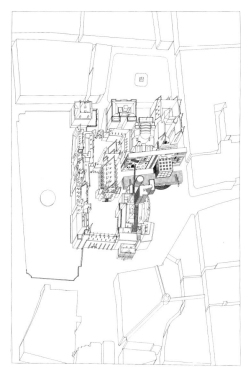

Project for the extension of
the Dutch Parliament,
The Hague, 1978

"The plan is of primary importance, because on the floor are performed all the activities of the human occupants." That formulation by Raymond Hood defines a "functionalist" architecture not obsessed by form, but one that imagines and establishes on the "floor" (i.e. the surface of the earth) patterns of human activity in unprecedented juxtapositions and catalytic combinations. OMA has been concerned with the preservation and revision of this tradition of so-called functionalism—exemplified by Leonidov, Melnikov, the "Berlin" Mies, the Wright of Broadacre City, the Hood of the Rockefeller Center—that was a campaign of territorial conquest for the programmatic imagination, so that architecture could intervene directly in the formulation of the *contents* of a culture, based on the givens of density, technology and definitive social instability.

Recent architecture has abandoned such claims.

Procrustes was the robber who made his victims fit his bed by stretching or lopping them. In the "new" historicist and typological architectures, culture will be at the mercy of a cruel Procrustean arsenal that will censor certain "modern" activities with the excuse that there is no room for them, while other programs will be revived artificially, simply because they fit the forms and types that have been resurrected.

In spite of the relentless criticisms concentrated on the insignificant episode of bastardized Modernism—it is essentially uncritical: it can only endorse the past.

Of the projects shown here, two are most pertinent for illustrating OMA's position, as in them the involvement with the past is more complicated.

The first is an intervention in a medieval Fortress (that had lost much of its authenticity through a series of restorations *à la* Viollet-le-Duc); the second a project for the renovation of a pure Panopticon, one of three ever built.

Both the Fortress and the Panopticon had to be equipped for their continuing operation in the 21st century: the Fortress with an extension of the Dutch Parliament that would proclaim the conquest of a former Royal Palace by democratic institutions, the Prison with a series of programmatic revisions that would adapt it to recent ideology. In such situations, both historicist and typological doctrine would represent artificial and unacceptable obstructions in a process of continuous cultural transformation that is desirable.

Only through the concrete projection of these revisions and their embodiment in tangible modernity can the weight of the past be made tolerable.

The significance of these two projects is in the way the past and modernity are related and made to coexist.

Otherwise, the wholesale desertion of the camp of utilitarian architecture opens an exhilarating prospect: that the field of modernity will be abandoned to create a condition where newness will be rare, intervention unusual, imagination shocking, interpretation subversive, and modernity once more exotic . . . an era of a new sobriety.

The Terrifying Beauty of the Twentieth Century
1985

Has any area in history—except perhaps the Forum in Rome—ever been richer in architectural history than the Forum des Halles and its immediate vicinity, including Beaubourg?

Here a whole urban region is now a seamless, almost Babylonian amalgam of destruction, kitch resurrections, authentic historical particles, a delirium of infrastructures, a mass grave of good and bad intentions, crawling from the pit like the rejected species of an alternative evolution. To what parallel Galapagos does this experiment belong? What of the culmination at La Défense, where all the geometrical rigor of a city collapses in a maelstrom of randomness and incoherence, made more pathetic by the profusion of roads, ramps and other "connections" that look like a wind-tunnel test accidentally executed in concrete? Yet, it mysteriously works or, at least, is full of people.

And what is the particular affliction that renders these treasures invisible, inaccessible, indigestible? Why are we all part of this ineffectual chorus that moans in the name of humanity about its culminating achievements? The 20th century ends on this note! Yes, Europe is now, almost everywhere, ridiculously beautiful for those who can forget—for a fleeting moment—the arbitrary delusions of order, taste and integrity. Its cities, through the objective agent of ideological mismanagement, are now exhaustive textbooks of flaws; the European Metropolis is like a reef on which each intention, each ambition, each solution, each question and each answer implacably run aground.

But like the forms that can be discovered in clouds, it is possible to will this landscape into an amazing spectacle of invention; read with the same concentration as the map of a treasure island, it reveals astonishing secrets.

One of the peculiar beauties of the twentieth century context is that it is no longer the result of one or more architectural doctrines evolving almost imperceptibly, but which represent the simultaneous formation of distinct archaeological layers; they result from a perpetual pendulum movement where each architectural doctrine contradicts and undoes the essence of the previous one as surely as day follows night. The resulting landscape needs the combined interpretative ability of Champoleon, Schliemann, Darwin and Freud to disentangle it.

Berlin/Rotterdam

Rotterdam and Berlin have much in common. Both historical centers, between the wars fertile grounds for their own specific modernities, then destroyed by the war; like Cain and Abel, the one good and the other bad. Then rebuilt in an atmosphere of optimism and thoughtless modernity, so pervasive that it became a vernacular. Now, today, both are caught in the grips of intense revisionism.

Berlin, first bombed, then divided, is centerless, a collection of centers sometimes nothing more than empty spaces. In Rotterdam, the bombs emptied the center; it was replaced by an artificial heart with emptiness as its core. In both cases, the current revisions are based on denial.

The richness of Berlin resides in the prototypical sequence of its models: neo-classical city, early Metropolis, modernist testbed, Nazi capital, war victim, Lazarus, cold war battlefield, and so on.

Now IBA is erasing this evidence, destroying in the name of history the very evidence of its destruction, which is exactly the most significant fact of its history (not to mention its aesthetics).

Rotterdam was the model city of the fifties, when the serene order of its slabs and the connective tissue of the Lijnbaan achieved paradigmatic status. In the sixties its popularity tumbled abruptly; in the end, only planning delegations from Eastern Europe and the third world came to visit. In the 1970s, new generations of planners took over. The old generation had simply been "building the city;" now that same city was declared a "gigantic problem." The unique quality of Rotterdam was the realization of openness at the scale of a whole center. Partly unintentional residue—simply the space around the slabs—this openness came under attack; plans were made for its densification or intensification, for the realization, even here, of the "compact city": intensification, as can only be expected from architects, in the form of material substance. They were blind to the mysterious qualities of this alleged void, first of all its unlimited freedom. Blind to the fact that the toddlers who could be seen—in the fifties—playing in the wading-pools at the foot of the slabs (happy evidence for the visiting tourists) had grown up and now formed a mutant urban herd, perfectly equipped to fill and exploit this post-modern plane where everything was possible and not a single social trope suppressed by architecture. That new patterns of migration had emerged: the trek from nowhere to nowhere as an exhilarating urban experience. Through the shift in urban ideology, they became a new kind of dispossessed: those chased from their modern habitat. May their numbers be limited in the coming decades!

The destruction of the center of Rotterdam during
World War II, and its reconstruction
with buildings by Marcel Breuer,
Van den Broek, and Bakema

Method

If there is a method in this work, it is a method of systematic *idealization;* a systematic overestimation of the *extant,* a bombardment of speculation that invests even the most mediocre aspects with retroactive conceptual and ideological charge. In this process, each bastard gets his own genealogical tree; the faintest hint of an idea is tracked with the obstinacy of a detective on a juicy case of adultery. If we pretend that our work will be implanted in an ideal world of intellectual prestige, artistic integrity and most importantly, seriousness, it will automatically acquire these same qualities, and remain as tangible manifestation of a theoretical perfection, long after the interpretative illumination of the author is removed? The mirror image of this action is the most clinical inventory of the actual conditions of each site, no matter how mediocre, the most calculating exploitation of its objective potential. This combined with a tempramental insistence on an almost scandalous—and literally unbelievable—simplicity that belies the complexity of the contextual interpretation, while at the same time doing justice to even its most delicate aspects. In some cases even providing the dignity of a retroactive concept is to exploit it objectively. In this manner, the interpretation of the Berlin wall as a park run through with a zen sculpture, made it possible to imagine the villas running along it. In Rotterdam, it was the banal conditions of water and traffic, together with the reductive inventory of modern typologies, that triggered the imagination. But maybe all these arguments are in the end mere rationalizations for the primitive fact of a taste for asphalt, traffic, neon, crowds . . . the very architecture of other people.

Imagining the Nothingness
1985

Maps of Berlin showing, clockwise from the bottom, the existing urban fabric, the city within the city, and a selection of urban archipelagos, from a seminar led by O. M. Ungers, Berlin, 1977

Clowns

Where there is nothing, everything is possible. Where there is architecture, nothing (else) is possible.

Who does not feel an acute nostalgia for those characters who could (even less than 15 years ago), with the vulgar stroke of a red pen, condemn—or was it liberate, after all?—whole areas of alleged urban desperation, change whole destinies, speculate seriously about the future through diagrams of untenable absurdity, leave whole auditoria panting with the doodles they left on the blackboard, manipulate politicians with savage statistics . . . bow ties the only external sign of their madness . . . the time when there were still . . . thinkers? In other words, we long for that whole histrionic branch of the profession that leapt like clowns, pathetic and courageous, from one cliff to another, flapping with inadequate wings but enjoying at least the free fall of pure speculation.

Maybe such nostalgia is not merely the longing for the former authority of this profession—nobody can seriously believe that architecture has lost any of its authority since its extinction—but also that for fantasy.

It is ironic that in architecture, "May 1968" has been translated only into more architecture: more pavement, less beach, even though many commendable activities take place independent of architecture.

Maybe the obstinacy of architects—a myopia that has lead them to believe that architecture is not only the vehicle of all that is good, but even the explanation of all that is wrong—is not merely a professional deformation but a reaction to the horror of architecture's opposite, that is: an instinctive recoil from the void, a fear of nothingness.

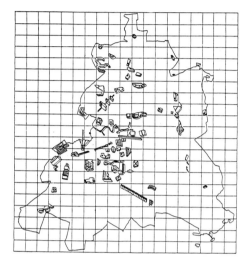
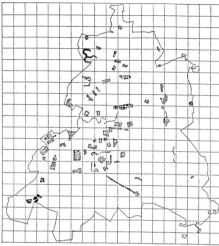
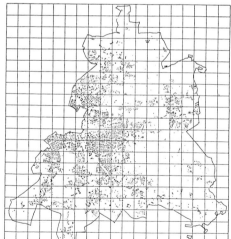

Berlin

Berlin is a laboratory. Its territory is forever defined and, for political reasons, can never be shrunk. Its population has declined continuously since the wall was built. It follows that fewer and fewer people inhabit the same metropolitan territory and take responsibility for its physical substance.

It could be assumed, boldly, that large areas of the city have ended up in ruins simply *because there is no longer any need for their existence.*

The blanket application of urban reconstruction in these circumstances may lead to their actual destruction—it may be as futile as keeping brain-dead patients alive with medical apparati.

What is necessary instead is to imagine ways in which the density can be maintained without recourse to substance, the intensity without the encumbrance of architecture.

In 1976, during a design seminar/studio led by O. M. Ungers, a concept was launched with implications that have not yet been recognized. "A Green Archipelago" proposed a theoretical Berlin, whose future was conceived in two diametrically opposite actions: the reinforcement of those parts of the city that warranted it and the destruction of those parts that did not.

This assertion contained the blueprint for a theory of the European metropolis, since it addressed its central ambiguity: the fact that many of its historical centers are in fact contained in metropolitan webs, that their urban facades merely mask the pervasive reality of the metropolis. In a model of urban solid and metropolitan void, the desire for stability and the need for instability are not incompatible. They can be pursued as two separate enterprises, tied by invisible connections.

Through the parallel actions of reconstruction and deconstruction, such a city becomes an archipelago of "architectural" islands floating in a post-architectural landscape or *erasure*, where what used to be city is replaced by a highly charged nothingness. The kind of coherence that the metropolis can achieve is not that of a homogeneous, planned composition. It can be, at the most, a system of fragments, a system of multiple realities; in Europe, the remnant of the historical core may well be part of such a system.

In the theoretical Berlin, "the green interspaces form a system of modified, sometimes artifical, nature . . . suburbs . . . parks . . . woods . . . hunting preserves . . . gardens . . . agriculture . . . The natural grid would welcome the full panoply of the technological age . . . highways, supermarkets, drive-in cinemas, landing strips, the ever-expanding video universe."

Nothingness here was to be a modified Kaspar David Friedrich landscape—a teutonic forest intersected by Arizona highways—in fact, a Switzerland.

Nevada

It is a tragedy that planners can only plan, and architects can only design further architectures. More important than the design of cities is, and certainly will be in the immediate future, the design of their decay. Only through a revolutionary process of erasure and the establishment of "free zones," conceptual Nevadas where the laws of architecture are suspended, will some of the inherent tortures of urban life—the friction between program and containment—be suspended.

If the most recent additions to the slagheap of history have landed there because their stylistic ugliness has made their true contents invisible, the exploration and cultivation of nothingness would explicate a hidden tradition.

Some hippies have been here before, the whole inarticulate horde of thinking members of the 1960s Anglo-Saxon counterculture—all the bubbles, domes, foams, the "birds" of Archigram (how bitter it will be to be rediscovered at the moment that amnesia has touched your own performance)—the philistine courage of Cedric Price.

Imaging nothing is:

Pompeii, city built with the absolute amount of walls and roofs;

The Manhattan Grid, "there" a century before there was a "there" there;

Central Park, void that provoked the cliffs that now define it;

Broadacre City, the Guggenheim, Hilberseimer's "Mid West"—with its vast plains of zero architecture;

The Berlin Wall . . .

They all reveal that this emptiness, the emptiness of the metropolis, is not empty, that each void can be used for those programs whose insertion in the existing texture is a Procrustean effort, leading to mutilation of both activity and texture. The projects for Amsterdam, but even more those for La Villette and the Universal Expositions, are attempts to imagine the quality of nothingness at the heart of the metropolis.

Architecture

Has there ever been another profession simultaneously in such good and bad shape as architecture in the past decade? More and more, architecture imposes on the world structures it never asked for.

From this follows its complete vulnerability: it is forever in the humiliating position of a lover enumerating his positive qualities to someone who has lost interest. Is there any connection to the fact that more or less at the moment that the world lost interest, the profession rediscovered architecture?

The rediscovery saw the birth of the jet-lagged avant-garde, the conferences, the shows, the publications—all of them demonstrating an interest that is somehow never translated in results, confidence, or respect. Somehow this circus is all cold fire, no sparks, sterile in its contributions to the mythology. In fact, the rediscovery had aspects of a self-help therapy—"Architecture Anonymous," a support group for people addicted to the same drug, compensating for a traumatic wound, trying to bolster their confidence through endless, ritualistic incantation of case histories.

At the same time, in Europe, political influences have completely infiltrated and attacked the core of architecture—disrupting its most intimate processes—in the form of a volatile climate of favors bestowed and withdrawn, support promised and denied, schedules compressed or expanded like an accordion stretched beyond tolerable limits at the whim of political seasons, financial impositions of a grotesque order, shameless reformulations of stated intentions, decisions swallowed inexplicably, cruel pleasure taken in the simple act of throwing away work for the sake of some higher but unexplained expediency; in other words, the state is

behaving like a malevolent Nature, whose meteorology knows only storms, cold fronts, cloudbursts . . .

In those countries where "participation" is institutionalized and has been enshrined in the law, the situation of the architect is even worse: sandwiched between the "top" and the "bottom," where the dilution of responsibilities leaves no one to be congratulated and no one to be blamed. An imposed preoccupation with the tactical permeates all these projects in their smallest details; but maybe it was always so: a sec-

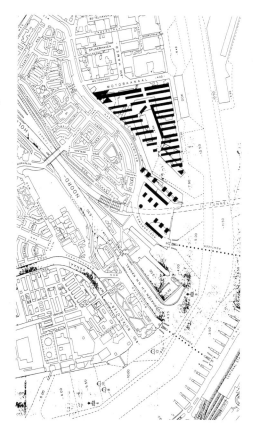

ond skin like scaffolding that disappears once the building is there. Sometimes, while driving near our site in Amsterdam, we witnessed housewives behind overloaded shopping carts who firmly dismissed specific architectural details that we had imagined bathed in an aura of sublime beauty, which, unfortunately will never be.[1] Or we find, on "our" territory, completely new appearances over which we have no control! It is increasingly difficult, in this climate of pervasive cynicism, to persuade and be persuaded. Inherent in this architecture is a bizarre, self-satisfied euphoria, strangely different from the rough treatment architects used to endure. The exquisite politeness and displays of highest civility serve only to mask the fact that there is no real discourse, that the debates are histrionic, the discussions rhetorical, the barbs blunted, the disagreements merely cosmetic. In the midst of such an excess of good manners, it is important to no longer act "cool," but to be gauche, dyspeptic, impassioned. Still, the relentless parading of the horrifying condition of architecture today—which could easily take on the proportions of Greek tragedy—can reveal the paradoxical fact that to be an architect today is to be one of the truly courageous heroes; the courage to alienate the client, to anger the patron, to lose favor with the politicians is necessary to the myth of architecture. Our cultural unconscious is hungry for tales of heroism, or at least for proof that certain essential things still exist, things that only an architect can accomplish.

1. Koolhaas refers to the IJ-plein project in Amsterdam-North.

The IJ-plein project,
Amsterdam-North, 1980–1989

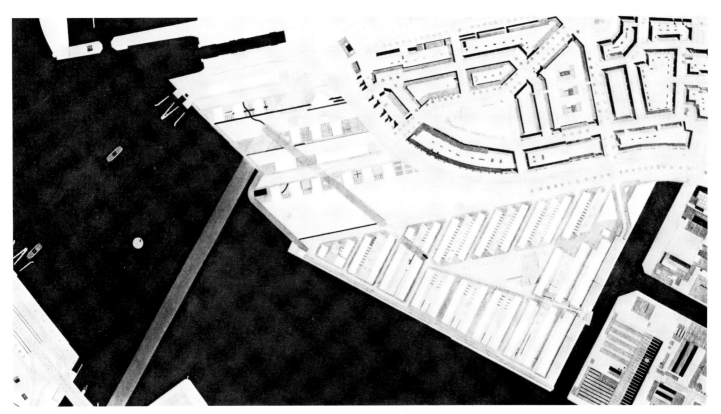

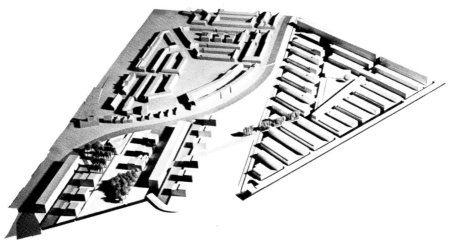

The permanence built into even the most frivolous item of architecture and the instability of the metropolis are incompatible.

In this conflict, the metropolis, by definition, will always win; in its pervasive reality architecture is reduced to the status of a plaything, tolerated as decor for the illusions of history and memory.

In Manhattan, this paradox is resolved in a brilliant way: through the development of a mutant architecture that combines the aura of monumentality with the performance of instability; its interiors accommodate "compositions" of program and activity that change constantly independently of each other without affecting what is called, with accidental profoundness, the envelope.

The genius of Manhattan is the simplicity of this split between appearance and performance: it keeps the illusion of architecture intact, while surrendering wholeheartedly to the exigencies of the metropolis; architecture is carried by the forces of the *Großstad* as a surfer is carried by the waves.

In the 1970s, architects wallowed in the capriciousness of authority.

Looking back at history, we see that not only did they rediscover old forms—a new erudition arrested at the first page of the history book: the door, the column, the architrave and the keystone—but also the symptoms of a former power and status. The endless axes, the impressive symmetries, the vast compositions, what were they if not the work of architects?

Inflated by nostalgic dreams of omnipotence, its erudition as much enriched as eroded by an obsession with form, the profession faced the end of the twentieth century in a confident mood. Ambiguous illustration of this fact were a series of great competitions—mass graves without paraphernalia: never has a single profession been so shamelessly drained of energy and money as architecture in the past fifteen years—each of them the potential beginning of a triumphal march toward a new kind of city, a new urbanity. In the first La Villette competition,[1] the architects were free to propose a whole new *quartier*, a fragment of the new more humane city of the future.

Offered the opportunity to imagine an ideal episode of late twentieth century life, hurtling *à toute vitesse* toward the third millenium, they imagined, finally, an environment fit for glass blowers and horse shoers, provided they drive a car with front-wheel drive. Later—emboldened by what?—this movement for the reconstruction of the European city became even more fanatical in the militancy of its declarations—shame on those who signed the Palermo declaration![2] Meanwhile, OMA, with a rigorous lack of timing, was totally absorbed in a twin preoccupation: the programmatic imagination— the simple interest in what happens—that seemed the unrealized object of a marginal band of modern architecture, and the phenomena of Manhattan, that seemed, in many ways, their accidental materialization. Their combination could define a plausible relationship between architecture, modernity, and the metropolis, their home base.

At La Villette, the second time around, the ingredients seemed there for a complete investigation of the potentialities of a metropolitan architecture in Europe: a *terrain vague* between the historical city—"raped" by the greedy needs of the twentieth century—and the plankton of the *banlieue*. On this terrain, two pieces of history sat rusting like marrooned spaceships:[3] a sort of nothing-

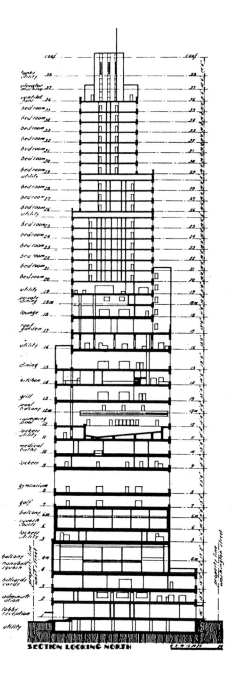

SECTION LOOKING NORTH

ness with still infinite potential, that in this case could be preserved since its program could not be expressed in form, a program that insisted on its own instability.

If the essence of *Delirious New York* was found in the section of the Downtown Athletic Club—a turbulent stacking of metropolitan life in ever-changing configurations—a machine that offered redemption through a surfeit of hedonism, a conventional, even boring skyscraper, and a program as daring as ever imagined in this century, La Villette could be still more radical by reducing the three-dimensional aspect almost entirely, proposing instead pure program, unfettered by any constraints. In this analogy, the bands across the site were like the floors of the tower, each program different and autonomous, but modified and "polluted" by the proximity of the others. The only stability was thus offered by the natural elements, the rows of trees and the Circular Forest—the forest machine—whose very growth insured their own instability. What La Villette finally suggested was the pure exploitation of the metropolitan condition: density without architecture, and a culture of "invisible" congestion.

1. Koolhaas refers to the competition for the Parisian Parc de la Villette in 1976.
2. The declaration of Palermo, published in 1978, was signed by Maurice Culot, Antoine Grumbach, Leon Krier, Pierluigi Nicolin, and Angelo Villa.
3. Koolhaas evokes here the Great Hall of La Villette and the old slaughterhouse transformed into the Museum of Science and Industry.

Sixteen Years of OMA

1988

Les charmes de l'horreur n'enivrent que les forts.
Charles Baudelaire,
Les Fleurs du Mal

The work presented here has been produced over the past sixteen years by a variety of people in several countries during two radically different cultural periods—the seventies and the eighties. This means that over the course of its existence, OMA has gone through several phases and responded to changing conditions.

The seventies

Exodus and the "American" work are products of the "visionary" sixties. In 1972 Archigram was at the height of its power and groups like Archizoom and Superstudio were conceiving architectural stories supposing a vast expansion of the territory of the architectural imagination.

Architecture then could be books, drawings, stories, and in some cases, even buildings. The tone of these productions was antihistorical, relentlessly optimistic and ultimately innocent.

"Exodus, or the Voluntary Prisoners of Architecture" was a reaction to this innocence: a project to emphasize that the power of architecture is more ambiguous and dangerous. Based on a study of "The Berlin Wall as Architecture," Exodus proposed to erase a section of central London to establish there a zone of metropolitan life—inspired by Baudelaire—and to protect this zone with walls from the old city, creating maximum *division* and *contrast*. The people of London could choose: those who wanted to be admitted to this zone of hyperdensity became "The Voluntary Prisoners of Architecture."

These two concepts—division and contrast—were also important for the study of Manhattan. The key project from this period is the City of the Captive Globe,

where the city is seen as an arena of competing ideologies—in which all conceptions of harmony and composition are considered as things of the past—and where the whole is an entity only to the extent that each part is different from every other.

Through the researches of *Delirious New York* the American work also became a polemic with the *utopian* aspect of European Modernism. The discovery of American architecture of the twenties and thirties is the discovery of a modernity that is a) built and b) popular.

In Europe the history of the twenties and thirties is a history of heroic but aborted dreams. Contrariwise, in twentieth-century American architecture, the twenties and thirties were rational revolutions, implemented by intelligent architects. It is not a catalog of frustration but an explosion of achievement, which—in spite of its realization—is as radical, imaginative and fantastic as the European dreams.

In the end—despite their non-realization— the projects for Manhattan and the book itself were aggressively realistic.

The eighties

At the end of the seventies, when OMA returned to Europe, the euphoria of the sixties—"Anglo-Saxon barbarism"—had been replaced by its opposite: architecture rediscovered history. In Europe this tendency led to "the rediscovery of the European cities" by the Krier brothers and other intellectuals and designers.

They were completely obsessed with the historic centers of Europe and apparently believed that the criteria applied to their construction were as valid today as they had been two or three hundred years ago. Their

activity threatened to completely deny, ignore—and ultimately repress—crucial aspects of the modern world such as scale, numbers, technology, programs, needs, that were at complete variance with their ideal of a "rediscovered" history.

This created a colossal reservoir of denial, which sought an outlet in the periphery of the cities, or which was pathetically masked to conform to the new dogmas and led to a mounting confusion between "real" and fabricated history.

In this light projects like the extension of the Dutch Parliament(1978), the Boompjes apartment building in Rotterdam (1980– 1982), the City Hall for The Hague (1986) or the housing at Koch-Friedrichstrasse in Berlin (1980) are polemical demonstrations that aspects of modernism, both American and European, can be made to co-exist with the historical core, and that only a new urbanism that abandons pretentions of harmony and overall coherence, can turn the tensions and contradictions that tear the historical city apart into a new quality. The projects celebrate the end of sentimentality.

Planning

In Europe the insistence during the seventies on the importance of the historical center and the urban fabric and the blanket critique of the whole post-war period led to the decline and eventual disappearance of an entire profession, that of planning, that critical form of imagination which pretends—in spite of obvious difficulties—to look forward, anticipate and organize needs before they become desperate. In this vacuum it was exiting to rediscover planning through projects such as the Parc de la Villette (1982-1983), the Universal Exposition

(1983), or Melun-Sénart (1987), in which questions beyond the strict domain of architecture could be initiated and developed. These projects are in fact quite far from architecture in the strict sens:; they deal with "nothingness." Where architecture answers, by definition, each question in the form of built substance, we tried in these projects to find forms of programmatic and organizational manipulation which could create new cultural conditions "free" of architecture. The most recent project in this series is the plan for Melun-Sénart, where the thesis of a city organized around its voids—a kind of post-architectural modernity—is tested.

The End of the Age of Innocence?

Destiny

Has there ever been a profession as incapable of defining and controlling its own destiny as that of architecture during the 1980s, at the moment of its apparent apotheosis? Offered to the public like the veritable fat lady in a museum of horrors, this discovery of architecture—by the media, developers, and museums—has devolved into a Faustian gambit now turned in on itself, drastically eroding the possibilities of architecture and progressively dismantling its ambitions.

Innocence

Delirious New York is an inquiry into the role architecture can play in modern culture. Hood, Harrison, and even Le Corbusier are interpreted in the book as the prototypes who document the complete mutation of the profession during the course of this century. Architects like Hood and Harrison seem to have had, in retrospect, an astonishingly direct relationship with their profession: it allowed them a pure materialization of collective forces, without a single afterthought. Where each European building is also commentary, theory, hesitation—all guarantees of profundity and subtlety—these American builders invented a different suspense: that of going directly to the goal.

Behind all admiration there is envy. I was jealous of my heros: like children who play with matches, they had innocently invented a style of living with Promethean obligations. "The Manhattan architects succeeded in their miracles by agreeing to a deliberate ignorance: it was now up to the architecture of the end of the twentieth century to assume *overtly* the pretensions and extravagant, megalomaniacal realizations of the metropolis."[1] The optimism of this text is synthetic: it be-

gins to apologize for the fact that the end of the twentieth century would be reduced to the themes and inventions of the early part of the century, and hides a doubt: if it is such a "constellation"—of urgency, of talent, of means, and naiveté—why does it never reproduce itself?

The 1980s

Here we are then in the 1980s. Our generation is supremely intelligent, well-informed, traumatized as it should be by certain cataclysms; architecture assumes (acknowledges) its dependence on other disciplines. A disproportionate part of its energy is used in constructing systems of impossibility—of order, coherence, invention, and innovation. The "Decon Show" in New York brought an opportune denouement to the 1980s with the cruel decision to consecrate an exhibition room to the "real" Soviet art of the 1920s—an effective demonstration of the lack of originality of the deconstructivists who were in fact the *raison d'être* of the show: after all, what could be more bizarre in *our* century than the similitude of works separated by a gap of seventy years?[2]

On a wall where the elements were literally glued, the projects of the 1920s, acting simply as a metaphorical wallpaper, unreal even when built, become pure commentary. Great progress in sophistication, tremendous loss in engagement (interaction?). After the Potemkin village, the Potemkin world.[3]

Chaos

In this perspective, how profound or pathetic is the discovery of chaos as a new inspiration? Chaos is only beautiful or interesting in as much as it represents the end of all deliberate intervention. Among all the

borrowings of this decade, chaos is the most paradoxical: seductive, but, *except among architects*, inaccessible.

The "butterfly effect" designates, in chaos theory, the axiom according to which a butterfly beating its wings in Japan will cause, perhaps, a cyclone in Cuba. In this equation the architect, more than any other, can be neither the butterfly nor the cyclone—neither cause nor effect.

His or her only possible contribution to chaos is to assume a role in the army of those who are vainly sworn to resisting it.

Parenthesis

A small disillusion: two successive trips to Japan, the first to study the Japanese city, that is to say, chaos, and the second to discover that the idea of chaos there is not only well documented and understood, but that it has already become an object for consumption. There, where intelligence meets masochism, chaos has rapidly become the dominant leitmotif of architecture and urbanism.

Melun-Sénart, Lille

At the end of the 1980s, we were faced with the sobering task of having to produce, in one year, projects for both Melun-Sénart and Lille.

The first developed, in a deliberate surrender—a tactical manoeuver to overturn a defensive position—this argument: if the built can no longer be controlled, it is rather the control of the void that should be sought— a new aesthetic of the city and new expectations followed from this idea. In the second, an extremely complex frame of infrastructure and of conceptual/financial speculations—how to imagine a place as important for the Japanese as for the Lillois—pushed

ineluctably toward the need for control. Like children whose parents force them to play with fire, we—intelligent, artists, architects—were astonished to be entrusted with the exact positioning of highways and the design of cloverleafs of eight levels of roads and railroad tracks. Was it not therefore a question of a showdown with bureaucrats of nerves more solid than our own? Or of others more competent, more experienced? Or of the generation before us?

Innocence II

The summer of 1989 was a logistical nightmare: three important competitions needed to be completed in three weeks: the marine terminal of Zeebrugge, a response to the imminent completion of the Channel; the Library of France in Paris; the Center for Art and Media Technology in Karlsruhe, an electronic "Bauhaus" conceived as a Darwinian arena in which art would be confronted with new technologies.

The simultaneous work on these three projects turned them into a family based on their enormous scale, their exceptional sites, their programs, and the fact that, in spite of their size, these buildings were nonetheless all devoted to collective activities.

The problem of the Big Footprint being posed seriously for the first time in Europe—it will be no doubt the theme of the end of the century—these competitions furnished the opportunity to explore the question of the Very Large Building—a type that proliferates effortlessly in North America, Japan, and South Korea, provoking a secret jealously among European architects—as well as the implications of the Vertical in Europe. Being "buildings of the third type," these projects provoked the unexpected resurrec-

tion of themes that formed the kernel of mutation of Manhattan architecture, whose discovery and exploration gave New York architects their most-inspired moments:
—the impossibility of organizing, with a single architectural gesture, a building disconnecting the autonomy of its parts
—the liberating potential of the elevator (through its ability to establish connections more mechanical than architectural) which allows architects to step outside traditional categories of composition
—the facade that can no longer divulge anything about the interior of the building, its center being too far removed from its skin. The idea of interior and exterior become two separate projects.
Finally, these buildings enter—by moving beyond the good and the bad—a dangerous domain, by the single fact of their size: their impact is wholly independent of their quality. Therefore, when we realized that we identified ourselves with these programmatic adventures that now occupy a radical position in the cultural and political landscape of Europe, we asked ourselves if, in playing for the first time in Europe with the fire of modernity, it would be possible to be again "innocent" in the face of architecture, and to imagine the end of the Potemkin world.

1. *Delirious New York*, 242.
2. Rem Koolhaas alludes to the exhibition "Deconstructivist Architecture," organized in 1988 by Philip Johnson and Mark Wigley. The work of Coop Himmelblau, Peter Eisenman, Frank Gehry, Zaha Hadid, Rem Koolhaas, Daniel Libeskind, and Bernard Tschumi was presented.
3. In *Spoken Into the Void*, Adolf Loos evoked these fictional villages, whose phantom facades were erected in the Russian countryside along the route of the czar.

Appendices

Biography

Rem Koolhaas was born in Rotterdam in 1944. From 1952 to 1956, he lived in Indonesia; he then moved to Amsterdam. Originally a journalist (for the *Haagse Post*) and a screenwriter, he studied architecture at the Architectural Association (AA) in London from 1968 to 1972.

From that period emerged two theoretical projects: "The Berlin Wall as Architecture," 1970, and, with Elia and Zoé Zenghelis and Madelon Vriesendorp, "Exodus, or the Voluntary Prisoners of Architecture," 1972. In 1972 he received a Harkness grant that allowed him to live and work in the United States for an extended period. He worked with Oswald-Mathias Ungers at Cornell University from 1972–1973, then was a visiting fellow at the Institute for Architecture and Urban Studies in New York, directed by Peter Eisenman; he held that post until 1979. He taught both at Columbia University and at UCLA. Beginning in 1976 he regularly returned to Europe, teaching at the AA and the University of Delft. At that time, Koolhaas was working on a study of New York, analyzing the impact of metropolitan culture on architecture. At the same time, he collaborated with Elia Zenghelis on several theoretical projects about New York: "The City of the Captive Globe," "Hotel Sphinx," "Welfare Palace Hotel," and "The Story of the Pool." The drawings from these projects were published in *Delirious New York: A Retroactive Manifesto for Manhattan*. A 1974 project for a house in Miami (with Laurinda Spear) won a *Progressive Architecture* award.

In 1975, Rem Koolhaas founded, with Elia and Zoé Zenghelis and Madelon Vriesendorp, the Office for Metropolitan Architecture (OMA), which sought to define new relationships—as much theoretical as practical—between architecture and the contemporary cultural situation.

The publication of *Delirious New York* in 1974 in New York, London, and Paris coincided with the "Sparkling Metropolis" exhibition at the Guggenheim Museum. One year later, Koolhaas organized a retrospective polemic about New York architect Wallace Harrison at the IAUS, entitled "Beyond Good and Evil." OMA's centers of interest have gravitated towards New York for theoretical work and Europe for practical work. Still in 1978, OMA—Zaha Hadid, Elia Zenghelis, Rem Koolhaas—entered a competition for an extension to the Dutch Parliament at The Hague, winning first prize *ex aequo*. This project would become the first of a series dedicated to the insertion of modern architecture into the difficult historical context of the European city. Following the urban studies and the competition for The Hague, OMA received several commissions in Holland: the development of the IJ-plein area of Amsterdam (comprising 1,375 apartments, a social center, and a school); the development of the quais along the Meuse in Rotterdam (the celebrated "slab tower" project); the renovation and expansion of a prison in Arnhem. Thus, in 1980, they opened an office in Rotterdam, which has subsequently become the main office. The Rotterdam office has centralized OMA's work, the majority of which is located in Holland (although they also have projects in Germany, France, Belgium, Switzerland, Japan, and the United States). The three principals in this office are Rem Koolhaas, Kees Christiaanse, and Ron Steiner.

In 1983, OMA took first prize—along with eight other entries—in a competition to design "an urban park for the twenty-first century" at La Villette in Paris. The project sought to define the pure forms of a metropolitan architecture, a chain reaction of events generated almost without building.

Starting in 1984, the French government invited OMA to propose an overall plan for a Universal Exhibition in Paris in 1989—a project later abandoned by its sponsors. The persistant interest in Rotterdam translated into an office tower project for Churchill-plein, and into the construction of a large bus shelter in front of the central station. With the National Dance Theater in The Hague, the projects take a polemical approach to the very nature of modernity and to the possible relationships between the volatile culture of the twentieth century, the metropolis, and architecture—research Rem Koolhaas supports with conferences around the world and numerous articles.

Several important projects will soon be completed, notably the Center for Art and Media in Karlsruhe, and an office complex in Frankfurt, although OMA did not win several important competitions (for the Dutch Architecture Center in Rotterdam, the French National Library in Paris, and the National School of Bridges and Highways in Marne-la-Vallée, France). Under Rem Koolhaas's direction, OMA is also intensifying new research on the new forms in European architecture in a project entitled "The Contemporary City." OMA's objective is to conceive, circulate, and realize its ideas about contemporary life in an international culture.

Twenty people—architects, technicians, and administrators—work at the Rotterdam office. The London studio focuses more on study projects. An office in Athens handles projects in Greece. Elia Zenghelis also practices independently and teaches in London. In addition to the three OMA offices, the Großstadt Foundation was created to concentrate specifically on "cultural" activities (publications, expositions, research, etc.), more easily executed and financed by a separate organization.

Chronology of works

1972
"Exodus, or the Voluntary Prisoners
of Architecture"
Project
"The City of the Captive Globe"
Project

1973
"The Egg of Columbus Circle"
New York, East River, United States
Project

1974
House
Miami, United States
Built (by Architectonica), 1976
(*Progressive Architecture* Award 1975,
with Laurinda Spear)

1975
Hotel Sphinx
New York, United States
Project
Development of Roosevelt Island
New York, United States
Competition
New Welfare Island
New York, United States
Competition

1976
"The Story of the Pool"
Project
Hotel Welfare Palace
New York, United States
Project

1978
Extension of the Dutch Parliament
The Hague, Netherlands
Competition (first prize *ex aequo*).
Renovation of a panoptic prison
Arnhem, Netherlands
Project

1979
Residence for the Prime Minister
Dublin, Ireland
Competition

1980
Social Housing
Kochstraße and Friedrichstraße,
Berlin, Germany
IBA Competition
Checkpoint Charlie
Berlin, Germany
IBA Competition
Social Housing
Lutzowstraße, Berlin, Germany
IBA Competition
IJ-plein
North Amsterdam, Netherlands
Study for a development plan
Construction of two buildings with
housing and public services:
–school, 1986;
–sporting facilities, 1987;
–boutiques, 1988;
–housing, 1988;
–social center, 1989;
–supermarket, 1989
"Slab Tower" and "Tower Bridge"
Rotterdam, Boompjes, Netherlands
Study

1981
Projects 1 and 2;
National Dance Theater
Scheveningen, Netherlands
Project 3;
The Hague, Netherlands
Built 1987

1982
Parc de la Villette
Paris, France
Competition

1983
Universal Exposition of 1989
East and West Sites
Paris, France
Study

1984
Offices at Churchill-plein
Rotterdam, Netherlands
Competition

Brink apartments
Gröningen, Netherlands
Built 1988
Villa Dall'Ava
Saint-Cloud, France
Built 1990
Two houses with patios
Rotterdam, Netherlands
Built 1988
Development plans
Cephalonia, Greece
Realized 1985
Police Commissariat
Almere, Netherlands
Built 1985
Development of public beaches
Skala, Greece
Study

1985
Morgan Bank
Amsterdam, Netherlands
Competition
Commuter station
Rotterdam, Netherlands
Competition: built 1987
Offices and restaurant
Amsterdam, Netherlands
Competition: built 1990
Reconstruction of the Bey of
Koutavos
Argostoli, Greece
Study
Parc Citroën-Cévennes
Paris, France
Competition

1986
Milan Triennial
Milan, Italy
Exhibit, casa Palestra
200,000th housing unit
The Hague, Netherlands
Exhibition, study plan director
Uithof 2000
Utrecht, Netherlands
Renovation and expansion of the Cité
Universitaire
Study

City Hall
The Hague, Netherlands
Competition
Bijlmermeer
Amsterdam, Netherlands
Urban renovation and redevelopment,
Study

1987
Scientopia, Science Park
Rotterdam, Netherlands
Study
Kunsthalle
Rotterdam, Netherlands
Competition: built 1991
Urban Planning Competition
New Town of Melun-Sénart, France
Competition

1988
Oosterflank offices
Rotterdam, Netherlands
Study
Archiparc offices
Utrecht, Rijnsweert, Netherlands
Study
Biocenter, laboratory for the Univer-
sity of Frankfurt, Germany
Competition

Apartment tower
The Hague, Netherlands
Study
Dutch Architectural Institute
Rotterdam, Netherlands
Competition
Hotel Furka Blick
Furka Pass, Switzerland
Built 1990
Euro-Disney
Marne-la-Vallée, France
Competition
Sports Museum
Flevohol, Netherlands
Study
International Business Center
Lille, France
Planning director, architect-in-chief
RWA (ateliers for handicapped people)
Amersfoort, Netherlands
Built 1990
Museum Park
Rotterdam, Netherlands
Built 1990

1989
Sea Trade Center
Zeebrugge, Belgium
Competition

International Housing Exhibition
Fukuoka, Japan
Built 1990
Office complex
Frankfurt, Germany
Competition, winning project
National Library of France
Paris
Competition
honorable mention
National Bridges and Roads School
Marne-la-Vallée, France
Competition
Center for Art and Media Techniques
Karlsruhe, Germany
Competition, winning project

1990
"Stad aan de Stroom"
Antwerp, Belgium
Hotel and Conference Center
Agadir, Morocco

1991
Project for the Congrexpo
Lille, France

Bibliography

Writings by Rem Koolhaas

"Exodus or the Voluntary Prisoners of Architecture" (with E. Zenghelis), in *Casabella* 378 (July 1973): 42–45.

"Ivan Leonidov's Dom Narkomtiazhprom" Moskva (with G. Oorthuys), in *Oppositions* 2 (January 1974): 95–103.

"Delirious New York," in *L'Architecture d'aujourd'hui* 186 (July 1976): 36–39.

"Roxy, Noah und die Radio City Music Hall," in *Archithèse* 18 (1976): 37–43.

"Bijlmermeer-strip," in *Werk-Archithèse* 64, no. 5 (May 1977): 17–19.

"Life in the Metropolis or the Culture of Congestion; The Story of the Pool/1976," in *Architectural Design* 47, no. 5 (May 1977): 319–325, 356.

"Architecture of the Planetary Metropolis Architectural Association, Diploma School: Unit 9," in *Lotus* 21 (1978): 7–17.

"Dali and Le Corbusier, the Paranoidcritical Method," in *Architectural Design* 48, no. 2–3 (1978): 153–163.

Delirious New York: A Retroactive Manifesto for Manhattan (New York: Oxford University Press, 1978); *New York délire, un manifeste rétroactif pour Manhattan* (Paris: Chêne, 1978).

"Radio City Music Hall: The Fun Never Sets," in *Wonen TABK* 11 (June 1978): 21–24.

"A Manifesto of Manhattanism: Delirious New York," in *Progressive Architecture* 59, no. 12 (December 1978): 70–75.

"Urban Intervention: Dutch Parliament Extension, The Hague," in *International Architect* 1, no. 3 (1980): 48–60.

"Town Planning and Delirium," in *Modo* 4, no. 30 (June 1980): 46–47.

"Nell'occhio del panopticon: rinnovamento del carcere di Arnhem" (with S. de Martino), in *Lotus* 32 (March 1981): 97–101.

"La rénovation d'une prison panoptique" (with S. de Martino);

"Un plan directeur pour Amsterdam–nord" (with J. Voorberg and H. De Kovel); "Deux structures pour Rotterdam" (with S. de Martino and K. Christiaanse), in *AMC Architecture Mouvement Continuité* 54–55 (June–September 1981): 60–75.

"Arthur Erickson vs. the All-Stars. The Battle of Bunker Hill" (with J. Wakefield et al.), in *Trace* 1, no. 3 (July–September 1981): 5–9.

"Project the the renovation of a Panopticon prison," in *Artforum* (September 1981): 41–43.

"OMA Projects 1978–1981," (London: The Architectural Association, 1981).

"Ein paar Bemerkungen zur Renovation des Kuppelgefängnisses von Arnhem," in *Archithèse* 11, no. 5 (September–October 1981): 41–46.

"Parc de la Villette: a Competition for a New Type of Urban Park. A Proposition in Two Phases: Hypotheses and Demonstration," in *UIA International Architect* 1 (1983): 32–37.

"Une Arcadie synthétique," in *L'Architecture d'aujourd'hui* 227 (June 1983): 96–99.

"Il parco del XX secolo," in *Casabella* 492 (June 1983): 12–18.

"Le contexte: la splendeur terrifiante du XX siècle; Urbanisme: imaginer le néant: Architecture: pour qui? Pourquoi?," in *L'Architecture d'aujourd'hui* 238 (April 1985): 15, 38, 71.

"Un angle de place. Agence de la banque Morgan, Amsterdam, Pays-Bas," in *L'Architecture d'aujourd'hui* 242 (December 1985): 53–57.

"Der Park als Bühne, die Natur als Schauspiel," in *Bauwelt* 77, no. 12 (March 1986): 415–417.

"OMA na het IJ-plein," in *IJ-plein*, catalogo (Amsterdam: Faculteit der Bouwkunde Technische Universiteit Delft & Stadsdeelraad Amsterdam-Noord, 1986): 3–10.

"Studieplan Koolhaas voor koepel in

Arnhem. Eerste aanezt tot amslag in het beleid," in *de Architect* 17, no. 5 (May 1986): 76–83.

"Maaskan prijs voor Koolhaas; De wereld is rijp voor de architect als visionair," in *Archis* 8 (August 1986): 45–47.

"Revisie Bijlmermeer" (with A. Zaayer, X. de Geyter, M. Guyer, Y. Brunier), in *Plan* 17, no. 4 (1987): 15–25.

"L'Institut hollandais d'architecture," in *Techniques & Architecture* 379 (August–September 1988): 40–42.

"Sixteen Years of OMA; From Delirious New York" (excerpts from *Delirious New York*), in *A + U* 217 (October 1988): 16–17, 135–150.

"Parisian Villa" (with X. de Geyter), in *Wiederhall* 9 (1988): 8–11.

"Une tour de Babel pas comme les autres; le Kunsthal de Rotterdam," in *Le Moniteur Architecture—AMC* 4 (September 1989): 22–30.

Writings on Rem Koolhaas and OMA

Abrams, J. "Paris Park Prize," in *Building Design* 624 (January 1983): 8.

———. "Delirious Visions," in *Blueprint* 44 (February 1988): 35–36.

Adang, M. "Gevangenisbouw in Nederland. De zin van de straf en de hoogte van de kosten," *Wonen TABK* 15 (August 1981): 6–26.

Allam-Dupré, E. "OMA—Rem Koolhaas, Habitations à IJ-Plein," in *AMC* 22 (October 1988): 54–61.

———. "Rem Koolhaas: Une gare maritime à Zeebrugge," in *Le Moniteur Architecture—AMC* 4 (September 1989): 20–23.

Baird, G. "Les extrêmes qui se touchent?" in *Architectural Design* 47, no. 5 (May 1977): 326–327.

Barbieri, U. "Dal ponte alla torre," in *Lotus* 47 (1985): 124–135.

———. "Il progetto domestico: de Triennale van Milaan," in *Items* V, no. 20 (1986): 28–33.

———. "Typen en prototypen van het wonen. De XVIIe Triennale van

Milaan," in *Archis* 3 (1986): 5–6

———. "Rem Koolhaas/OMA: Teatro olandese di danza," in *Domus* 689 (December 1987): 44–55.

Barbieri, U. and R. van Duivenbode. "Costruzione e progetto," in *Casabella* (September 1985): 12–13.

Barbieri, U. and M. Zardini. "Due progetti per il municipio dell'Aja," in *Casabella* 539 (October 1987): 39–41.

Beck, H. "Towards an Architecture of Congestion," in *Express Extra* 1, no. 2 (1982): 3.

van de Beek, J. "Woontorens OMA markeren omslag in Gröningen Grootschalig element aan Verbindingskanaal," in *de Architect* 19, no. 12 (December 1988): 73–77.

Bekaert, G. "De odyssee van een verlicht ondernemer," in *Wonen TABK* 13–14 (July 1982): 50–57.

———. *De verteller. Office for Metropolitan Architecture* (Antwerp: Antwerpen, tentoonstellingscatalogus de Singel, 1988).

———. "Gesprekken over glasoverkapte ruimten," in *Bouw* 9 (4 May 1990): 11.

Bergh, R. and J. Rutten. *De Fascinatie van Hooghouw* (Rotterdam: Uitgeverij 010, 1985): 30–39.

Jones, P. Blundell. "Von der gefährlichen Schönheit und der surrealistischen Schönheit," in *Bauwelt* 80, no. 1–2 (January 1989): 40–49.

Boekraad, C. "De invloed van Mies van der Rohe," in *Archis* 3 (March 1987): 26–29.

de Boer, H. "Het uur der waarheid. De juryuitslag voor de theorie en tegen het landschap?" in *Contour* 2 (September 1983): 24–29.

de Boer, H. and H. van Dijk. "Het Park van de 21ste eeuw," in *Wonen TABK* 12 (June 1983): 8–29.

de Boer-Kommers, M. and W. Droogleever Fortuyn. "Pleidooi voor een ruimere stedebouwkundige visie," in *Bouw* 36, no. 22 (October 1981): 29–31.

O. Boissière, "La Haye, le théâre de

la danse," in *L'Architecture d'aujourd'hui* 257 (July 1988): 28–33.

Bollerey, F. " . . . immer wieder eine Mischung von Verführung und Ungeniessbarkeit ins Spiel bringen," in *Bauwelt* 78, no. 17–18 (May 1987): 627–663.

_____. "Het Ideaal van de Metropolis," in *Beeld* 2, no. 4 (February 1987): 8–13.

_____. "El linterespor lo artificial: Conversacion con Rem Koolhaas," in *Architectura Viva: Hollanda Domestica* 19 (1989): 18–23.

Bosma, K. "Van individuele dressuur naar collectief tijdverdrijf: renovatie van de Koepel in Arnhem," in *de Architect* 17 (May 1986): 85–90.

_____. "De Architect die de leegte bouwde. OMA's stedebouwkundige concepten binnen het krachtenspel van de verstedeljking," in *Archis* 3 (March 1989): 46–51.

Bosma, K. and H. van Dijk. "Ik ben nu al zeker drie jaar bezig om dat stigma van het moderne van me af te schudden, juist omdat het in Nederland zo gemakzuchtig wordt beleden," interview with Rem Koolhaas, in *Archis* 3 (March 1989): 42–45.

Boudet, D. "Karlsruhe: Centre des Arts et des Technologies," in *Le Moniteur* 8 (February 1990): 12–13.

Bouman, T., T. Visser, and H. Hekkema. "Interview met Rem Koolhaas," in *Contour* 2 (June 1984): 4–13.

Boyer, C.-A. "Entretien: Koolhaas: Dessiner entre indétermination et spécificité," in *L'Architecture d'aujourd'hui* 269 (June 1990): 34, 39.

Brandolini, S. "Il Teatro olandese di danza all'Aja," in *Casabella* (September 1985): 4–11.

Breton, G. "Rem Koolhaas: Théâtre de Danse la Haye 1987," in *Théâtres* (Paris: Editions du Moniteur, 1989): 54–63.

Brouwers, R. *Zes ontwerpen voor het Nederlands Architectuurinstituut* (Amsterdam: Nederlands Architectuurinstituut, 1988).

Bru, E. and J. L. Lluis Mateo. *Arquitectura europea contemporánea* (Barcelona: Editorial Gustavo Gili, 1987): 70–73.

Buchanan, P. "A.A. Now: Celebration and Comparison," in *The Architectural Review* 1040 (October 1983): 44–47, 68–76.

_____. "Rotterdam Rationalists," in *The Architectural Review* 1055 (January 1985): 45–47.

_____. "OMA at The Hague," in *The Architectural Review* 1084 (June 1987): 87–91.

_____. "Three Dutch Architects," in *AA Files* 16, (Autumn 1987): 7–22.

_____. "Koolhaas Container," in *The Architectural Review* 1099 (September 1988): 32–39.

_____. "Actualidad de una tierra artificial," in *Architectura Viva* 19 (1989): 4–11.

van der Cammen, H. *2050 Nieuw Nederland Onderwerp van ontwerp deel II Beeldverhalen* (The Hague: Staatsuitgeverij, 1987): 35–37.

Campo, M. "Architectuur?" in *Futura* 15, no. 5 (1980): 3–12.

Casciato, M. and A. Aymonino. "Edifici residenziali e scuola, IJ-plein," in *Domus* 702 (February 1989): 29–39.

Casey, C. and M. Mathewson. "Die Inszenierung der Metropole," in *Bauwelt* 80, no. 1–2 (January 1989): 15–33.

Cervello, M. "Interview with Rem Koolhaas," in *Quaderns* 183 (October–December 1989): 79–103.

Christiaansen, J. H. "Hollandsk arkitekturpris til Koolhaas," in *Arkitekten* (DM) 88, no. 18 (October 1986): 428–429.

Collee, J. *Hoog in Nederland; een onderzoek naar de motieven achter hoogbouw* (Amsterdam: Kunsthistorich Instituut van de Universiteit van Amsterdam, 1986).

Cook, P. "Unbuilt England," in *AMC* 10 (October 1987): 52–55.

Damisch, H. "Cadavre exquis," in *AMC* 18 (December 1987): 21–22.

van Dansik, D. "Bijlmer en Uithof door het OMA geanalyseerd. Studies voor de vitaliseriing van de stedebouw," in *de Architect* 25 (December 1986): 25–31

_____. "Le project d'OMA pour Amsterdam," in *Urbanisme* 219 (May 1987): 80–88.

_____. "Stadhuis Bibliotheek Den Haag. Viif plannen voor een moeilijke locatie," in *de Architect* 18 (January 1987): 26–33.

Daru, M. "Het functionalisme is niet dood want het heeft nog tegenstanders," in *Plan* 8, no. 4 (April 1977): 7–31.

Devolder, A. M. *Tracé spoortunnel. Negen Concepten. Railway Tunnel Site. Nine Concepts* (Rotterdam: Uitgeverij 010, 1988).

Dietsch, D. K. "Modern Romance: Eight Projects by the Office for Metropolitan Architecture," in *Architectural Record* 176, no. 3 (March 1988): 94–107.

_____. "First Position," in *Architectural Record* 176, no. 4 (April 1988): 72–81.

van Dijk, H. "Rem Koolhaas: de reincarnatie van de moderne architectuur; Rem Koolhaas interview," in *Wonen TABK* 11 (June 1978): 7–16, 17–20.

_____. "Demokratische Symbolik oder Architektur?" in *Werk-Archithèse* 25–26 (1979): 7–11.

_____. "Het bezwijken van tegenstellingen," in *Wonen TABK* 13–14 (July 1982): 13–45.

_____. "Rem Koolhaas: Architectonic Scenarios and Urban Interpretations," in *Dutch Art & Architecture Today* 12 (December 1982): 20–27.

_____. "OMA krijgt opdracht Churchill-pleintoren," in *Wonen TABK* 20 (1984): 2.

_____. "Ambitie op zoek naar een 'kritische massa.' OMA's nederlands Dans theater in Den Haag," in *Archis* 4 (April 1988): 36–43.

_____. "Zes architecturen op zoek naar een opdrachtgever. De ontwerpen voor het Nederlands Architectuurinstituut," in *Archis* 7 (July 1988): 8–21.

_____. "Den complete stad geamendeerd. Negen visies op het Roterdamse spoortunneltracé," in *Archis* 11 (November 1988): 28–35.

_____. *Architectuur in Nederland jaarboek 87–88*, Van Loghum Slaterus (December 1988).

_____. "De verovering van de wansmaak en de laagte. De architectuur van Koolhaas' kleine projecten," in *Archis* (March 1989): 13–26.

Fisher, T. "In the Dutch Modernist Tradition (Patio Villa, Kralingen)," in *Progressive Architecture* (December 1989): 86–89.

_____. "Logic and Will (IJ-Plein Housing)," in *Progressive Architecture* (March 1990): 96–101.

_____. "Projects: Rem Koolhaas (Sea Terminal Zeebrugge, Très Grande Bibliothèque, Media Center Karlsruhe)," in *Progressive Architecture* (April 1990): 123–125.

Frampton, K. "Two or Three Things I Know about Them: A Note on Manhattanism," in *Architectural Design* 47, no. 5 (May 1977): 315–318.

Fortier, B. "La Grande Ville: un entretien avec Rem Koolhaas," in *L'Architecture d'aujourd'hui* 262 (April 1989): 90–103.

Futagawa, Y. "Office for Metropolitan Architecture, Project 1: Townhall, The Hague; Project 2: Dance Theatre, The Hague," in *GA Document* 18 (April 1987): 45–51.

_____. ed., "Office for Metropolitan Architecture: Villa Kralingen, Rotterdam, The Netherlands," in *GA Houses* 27 (November 1989).

Geurtsen, R. and N. Koknich. "Gröningen onder supervisorien. Stadsontwerp intensiveringszone Verbindingskanaal," in *de Architect*

XIXI, no. 4 (April 1988): 36–50.

Goulet, P. "Concours international pour le parc de la Villette," in *L'Architecture d'aujourd'hui* 227 (June 1983): 90–91.

_____. "La deuxième chance de l'architecture moderne; entretien avec Rem Koolhaas; . . . ou le début de la fin du réel; entretien avec Elia Zenghelis," in *L'Architecture d'aujourd'hui* 238 (April 1985): 2–9, 10–14.

Goulet, P. and N. Kunhert. "Die erschreckende Schönheit des 20. Jahrhunderts," in *Arch* + 86 (August 1986): 34–43.

de Graaf, R. "Laissez faire: planvorming voor het Amsterdamse GEB-terrein," in *Wonen TABK* 16–17 (1985): 6–7.

_____. "Strip toren en villa's: de plannen van OMA voor Amsterdam Zuid-Oost," in *Archis* 11 (November 1987): 30–35.

Graafland, A. *Esthetisch vertoog en ontwerp: Theorie en methode van betekenisverlening in architectuur en kunst* (Nijmegen: Uitgeverij Sun, 1986): 138–154.

Griffen, M. "Prime Minister's Residence," in *International Architect* 1, no. 4 (1981): 6–7.

Groothoff, M. C. "Spuitheater Den Haag geopend. Contrast muziek; en danstheater een verademing, in *Arcade* 1 (October 1987): 8–21.

van Hezik, M. "Van Berlage to Bijlmer en weer terug," in *de Architect* 12, no. 12 (December 1981): 44–53.

den Hollander, J. "Rem Koolhaas over symbolen in de architectuur," in *de Architect* 10, no. 3 (1979): 58–59.

Hubeli, E. "Metropolitane Erzählungen: Rem Koolhaas, Architekturprogrammatik und Projekte vom Office for Metropolitan Architecture," in *Werk, Bauen + Wohnen* 5 (May 1987): 37—39.

Iden, P. "Auf der Suche nach der Figur," in *Bauwelt* 80, no. 1–2 (January 1989): 34–39.

Jencks, C. "Irrationeel rationalisme.

'The rats' sinds 1960, in *Panorama van de Avant-gardes*" (Arnhem: Academie Arnhem Pers, 1981): 12–27.

_____. "Die Architektur der Dekonstruktion—Die Freuden des Absens," in *Arch* + 96–97 (November–December 1988): 30–33.

Jonker, G. "Een bruuske uitspraak uit de Nieuwe Hopeloosheid," in *Bouw* 35, no. 24 (November 1980): 24–25.

Jonker, N. and G. J. de Rook. *Het Haagse stadhuis centraal*, catalog, (The Hague: Gemeentemuseum, 1986): 20–23.

Karssenberg, A. "Politiebureau te Almere-Haven," in Bouw 42, no. 2 (January 1987): 18–19.

ten Kate, G. "Verkeersgebouw te Rotterdam," in *Bouw* 42, no. 22 (October 1987): 21–24.

Kegel, R., F. Schokkenbroek, and C. M. Steenbergen. *Parc de la Villette; concours international, Paris, 1982* (Delft: Nederlandse inzendingen Delfste Universitaire Pers, 1983): 47–54.

Kloos, M. *Amsterdam, An Architectural Lesson* (Amsterdam: Thoth, 1988): 109–118.

Klotz, H. *Revision der Moderne: Postmoderne Architektur 1960–1980* (Munich: Prestel Verlag, 1984): 206–217.

_____. "Vision of the Modern OMA: Parc de la Villette," in *Journal of Architectural Theory & Criticism* (USA, ed. Gran Bretagna) 1, no. 1 (1988): 66–71.

Koek, R. "Rotterdam werkt aan stedelijke indentiteit. Ontwerpen voor pleineen en spoortunneltracé," in *de Architect* 19, no. 10 (October 1988): 40–47.

de Koning, M. "De economie van de verbeelding," in *Vlees & Beton* 4 (October 1985).

Kuhnert, N., ed. "Rem Koolhaas: Delirious New York, Rem Koolhaas im Gespräch mit Arch +, Rem Koolhaas: Das Atlanta-Experiment, Antwerpen: Stadt gegen Peripherie, Melun Sénart, Zentrum für Kunst

und Medientechnologie Karlsruhe," in *Arch* + 105–106 (October 1990): 59–83.

Lambert, D. "Het Stadsontwerp aan het IJ. Planvorming rond het Oosterdok in Amsterdam," in *Archis* 7 (July 1987): 10–19.

Lampugnani, V. Magnago. "Il caso Gröningen," in *Domus* 695 (June 1988): 48–55.

Latham, I. "Polyrationalism at the RIBA, Review of the Week-long Symposium," in *Building Design* 645 (June 1983): 6–7.

_____. "Six of the Best for Rotterdam," in *Building Design* 900 (February 1988): 22–23.

Lefaivre, L. "Dirty Realism in der Architektur," in *Archithèse* (January–February 1990): 14–21.

Leupen, B. *IJ-plein catalogus* (Amsterdam-Noord: Faculteit der Bouwkunde Technische Universiteit Delt/Stadsdelraad, 1986).

_____. "Het IJ-plein in de traditie van de moderne woningbouw," in *de Architect* 19, no. 3 (March 1988): 51–59.

_____. *IJ-plein, Rem Koolhaas/OMA, Een speurtocht naar nieuwe compositorische middelen* (Rotterdam: Ultgeverij 010, 1989).

_____. ed. *Hoe Modern is de Nederlandse Architectuur?* (Rotterdam: Uitgeverij 010, 1990).

Leupen, B. and N. Bisscheroux. *IJ-plein diktaat* (Delft: Technische Universiteit, 1983).

Loriers, M. C. "Sur la crête de la vague moderne" and "Théâtre de la danse, La Haye," in *Techniques & Architecture* 380 (October–November 1988): 76–77, 78–87.

Loof, M. and J. van Stigt "Form follows fancy. Het populaire modernisme van Arquitectonica," in *Archis* 4 (April 1988): 16–25.

Looise, W. "Inspraak IJ-plein," in *Oase* 17 (estate 1987): 35–37.

Lootsma, B. "OMA's strategieën," in *Forum* XXLX, no. 3 (1985): 124–131.

_____. "De Onzichtbaren," in *Forum* 31, no. 1 (1987): 36–43.

Lucan, J. " Auf dem Kamm der Welle," in *Bauwelt* 80, no. 1–2 (January 1989): 50–53.

Maas, T. "Vijf ontwerpen voor een groot-stedelijk kantoorgebouw," in *de Architect* 15, no. 11 (November 1984): 30–33.

Macgowan, T. "The Parc de la Villette, Paris; Twentieth century Theory for the Twenty-first Century Urban Park," in *Landscape Australia* 6, no. 1 (February 1984): 19–35.

Mangin, D. "Amsterdam, le IJ-plein de Rem Koolhaas et de l'OMA," in *L'Architecture d'aujourd'hui* 257 (July 1988): 12–21.

Mateo, J. L., ed. *Rem Koolhaas: Projectes Urbans 1985–1990* (Barcelona: Collegi d'Arquitectes de Catalunya/Quaderns Monografies, 1991).

Meijer, J. and E. Tee, eds. *What a Wonderful World: Music Videos in Architecture* (Gröningen: Gröninger Museum/Dienst Ruimtelijke Ordening Gemeente, 1990): 58–63.

Mens, R. "Villa-architectuur van naam in de Bijlmermeer," in *de Architect* 17, no. 7–8 (July–August 1986): 53–55.

Merkel, J. "Not so Delirious Modernism," in *Art in America* (April 1988): 27–33.

_____. "Architectural Traveler: Past-Present-Future Tense in Rotterdam," in *Inland Architecture* 34, no. 3 (May–June 1990): 99–102.

Metcalf, A. and G. Baird, "Graves, Koolhaas and Baird in Australia," in *International Architect* 4 (1981): 4–5.

Metz, T. "Design Awards/Competitions; Competition for a New City Hall in The Hague, Holland," in *Architectural Record* 175, no. 4 (April 1987): 54–55.

Meuwissen, J. "Delirious Rotterdam," in *Plan* 13, no. 2 (February 1982): 8–9.

_____. "Architectuur in Rotterdam," in *Plan* 16, no. 7–8 (August 1985): 41–44.

_____. "Autobiographical Architecture: Some Introductory Remarks," in *Wiederhall* 9 (1988): 6–7.

Monninger, M. "Erfinder am Reissbrett," in *Frankfurter Allgemeine Magazin* fasc. 550 (14 September 1990): 12–40.

von Moos, S. "Rotterdam lädt Leonidow ein," in *Archithèse* 11, no. 5 (September–October 1981): 57–62.

_____. "Dutch Group Portrait," in *A + U* 217 (October 1988): 86–95.

_____. "Hollands groepsportret. Aantekeningen over het ontwerp van OMA voor het stadhuis in Den Haag," in *Archis* 3 (March 1989): 27–33.

Morris Dixon, J. "Architectural Design: Agreeing to Disagree," in *Progressive Architecture* (January 1975): 44–47.

_____. "Layers of Meaning," in *Progressive Architecture* (December 1979): 66–71.

Neitzke, P. *Jahrbuch für Architektur* (Braunschweig: Vieweg & Sohn Verlag, 1988): 88–109.

Neumeyer, F. "Metropolitan Interface; OMA's project für Euralille," in *Archithèse* (January–February 1990): 44–49.

_____. "OMA's Berlin: The Polemic Island in the City," in *Assemblage* 11: 37–53.

Niesten, J. "Prijsvraag uitbreiding Tweede Kamer: Meerdere inzendingen een volgende ronde waard," in *de Architect* 9, no. 11 (November 1978): 40–45.

Noviant, P. "Un Européen sans humour," in *AMC* 54–55 (June–September 1981): 59.

Noviant, P. and B. Vayssière, "L'indétermination et la foi," in *AMC* 6 (December 1984): 30–31.

Papadakis, A. C. and E. Zenghelis, "OMA: Houses in Antiparos," in *Architectural Design* 51, no. 6–7 (1981): 58–63.

Peake, C. "The Pleasure of Architecture Conference, 1980, Syndney, Australia," in *Transition* 1, no. 4 (November 1980): 4–23.

Peters, P. "IBA 1987: Wohnungsgrundrisse—Ort—Typologie Analyse Multiplizierte Wohnungen," in *Baumeister* 84, no. 5 (May 1987): 32.

Polak, M. *Het creatief ontwerp in architektuur & stedebouw: een psychodynamisch kritische benadering* (Delft: Delftse Universitaire Pers, 1984): 268.

Porphyrios, D. "Pandora's Box: An Essay on Metropolitan Portraits," in *Architectural Design* XLVII, no. 5 (May 1977): 357–362.

Postel, D. "Werk in uitvoering. Woningbouw van OMA op het IJ-plein," in *de Architect* 19, no. 6 (June 1988): 68–75.

Raggi, F. "Puritan-hedonist," in *Modo* 7, no. 58 (April 1983): 26–28.

Rödermond, J. "Over het onvermogen van architecten," in *de Architect* 11, no. 12 (December 1980): 54–61.

_____. "Interbau Berlin 1984 Koolhaas Berlijns Pompei," in *de Architect* 12, no. 6 (June 1981): 41–53.

_____. "Bestemmingsplan ADM-terrein Amsterdam," in *de Architect* 13, no. 10 (1982): 84–95.

_____. "Het park van de 21ᵉ eeuw. Prijsvraag park la Villette te Parijs," in *de Architect* 14, no. 3 (March 1983): 44–49.

_____. "Lichtvoetig OMA-ontwerp voor Nederlands danstheater in Scheveningen," in *de Architect* 15, no. 4 (April 1984): 33–37.

_____. "De stad als kunstwerk of als banaliteit? IJ-plein en Venserpolder," in *de Architect* 15, no. 10 (1984): 45–55.

_____. "OMA, gaat bouwen. Terughoudende vormgeving in recent werk," in *de Architect* 16, no. 9 (September 1985): 93–99.

_____. "Prijsvraag standaard celindeling. Het zoeken naar een optimale oplossing voor tegenstrijdige eisen met een minimaal budget," in *de Architect* 17, no. 6 (June 1986): 67–71.

_____. "Politiebureaus in Landgraaf en Almere," in *de Architect* 17, no. 7–8 (July–August 1986): 42–49.

_____. "Nederlands danstheater. Een uitermate utilitair gebouw," in *de Architect* 18, no. 10 (October 1987): 73–79.

_____. "Toekomst europese stad ter discussie tijdens symposia in Delft en Maastricht," in *de Architect* 19, no. 6 (June 1988): 49–55.

_____. "Zes ontwerpen voor een Architectuurinstituut," in *de Architect* 19, no. 7–8 (July–August 1988): 29–41.

_____. "Architectenkeuze Architectuurinstituut: ondoorzichtige besluitvorming," in *de Architect* 19, no. 11 (November 1988): 32–33.

Rutten, J. "Rem Koolhaas: Congestie voor mij interessanter dan Hoogbouw," in *Bouw* 4 (16 February 1985): 21–24.

_____. "Stadhuis en Bibliotheek Den Haag," in *Bouw* 26, (20 December 1986): 12–28.

Santi Gualtieri, E. and U. Barbieri. "Amsterdam IJ-plein," in *Abitare* 236 (July–August 1985): 54–55.

Schilperoord, J. "Konstruieren. Dimensionierung und Detaillierung eines Schalendaches am Stationsplein in Rotterdam," in *Deutsche Bauzeitung* 121, no. 10 (October 1987): 48–50.

Skude, F. "Modificeret Modernism," in *Arkitektur* (DK) 7 (October–November 1988): 160–164.

Steigenga, M. "Kleerscheuren," in Forum 31, no. 2 (1987): 2–5.

Stoutjesdijk, H. "Plannan voor de Drievriendenhof, Dordrecht: Benthem & Crowel favoriet in matige competitie," in de Architect 17, no. 9 (September 1986): 65–67.

Sudjic, D. "The Superstars of the Office for Metropolitan Architecture," in *Building Design* 549 (12 June 1982): 2.

_____. "Carta desde Fukuoka: La 'mini-IBA' de Isozaki," in *Architectura Viva* 11 (March–April 1990): 50–52.

Tonka, H. *Architecture & Cie* 1 (Arc et Senans: Les Editions du Demicercle, Autumn–Winter 1988).

Tschumi, Bernard. "On Delirious New York: A Critique of Critiques," in *International Architect* 1, no. 3 (1980): 68–69.

Vayssière, B., P. Noviant, and J. Lucan. "Rem Koolhaas entretien," in *Architecture Mouvement Continuité* 6 (December 1984): 16–21.

Vermeulen, P. "Sleutelen aan het Antwerpse trauma," in *Archis* (September 1990): 46–51.

Verwijnen, J. "Rem Koolhaas ja Office for Metropolitan Architecture OMA," in *Arkkitehti* (Finland) 85, no. 5 (June 1988): 30–43.

Vidler, Anthony. "The Office for Metropolitan Architecture," in *Skyline* (May 1982): 18–21.

_____. "De ironie van metropolis," in *Wonen TABK* 13–14 (July 1982): 46–49.

Voorberg, J. "Tweede Kamerprijsvraag: pleidooi voor Koolhaas," in *Wonen TABK* 13 (July 1980): 2–3.

de Vreeze, N. "Een Koolhaas als salles promotion," in *Archis* 12 (December 1988): 6—7.

Wakefield, J. and R. Koolhaas. "Arthur Erickson vs. the 'All-Stars': The Battle of Bunker Hill," in *Trace* 1, no. 3 (July–September 1981): 9–15.

Wall, A. "La Villette competition: The Programme for a New Type of Park," in *UIA International Architect Magazine* 1 (1983): 26.

Welling, H. G. *Udviklinger i byfornyelsens arkitektur* (Copenhagen: Kunstakademiets Arkitektskole, 1987).

Welsh, J. "Rostrum: Last Stop on a Grand Tour," in *Building Design* 957 (13 October 1989): 2.

Wiegersma, L. W. "Parc de la Villette: een unieke prijsvraag," in *Plan* 14, no. 2 (February 1983): 8–12.

Wilson, P. "The Park and the Peak—Two International Competitions," in *AA Files* 4 (July 1983): 76–79.

Wolf, D. *Architectuuropgave Drievriendenhof; Dordrecht 1986*

(Dordrecht: Commissie Kunst & Architectuur, 1986): 42–43.

Wyatt, G. "Koolhaas and OMA win The Hague City Hall Competition," in *Progressive Architecture* (April 1987): 27–28.

Zaera, A. "Conceptual Evolution of the Work of Rem Koolhaas," in *Rem Koolhaas: Projectes Urbans 1985–1990,* (Barcelona: Collegi d'Arquitectes de Catalunya/Quaderns Monographies, 1991).

Zanoni, T. "Precedent and Invention: Design in the Field of Tension," in

Harvard Architectural Review 5 (1986): 172–187.

_____. "Wettbewerbsprojekt Stadthaus Den Haag, December 1986," in *Werk, Bauen + Wohnen* 5 (May 1987): 40–46.

van Zeijl, G. "Koolhaas, Weeber en het nieuwe nut," in *Plan* 15, no. 11 (November 1984): 38–39.

Zenghelis, E. "Arcadie. Le paradis transposé," in *L'Architecture d'aujourd'hui* 238 (April 1985): 55.

_____. "The Aesthetics of the Present," in *Architectural Design* 58, no.

3–4 (March–April 1988): 66–67.

Zgustova, M. and L. Vacchini, "Office for Metropolitan Architecture," in *Quaderns* 173 (April–June 1987): 2–125.

Zwinkels, C. "Meervoudige opdracht levert niet de gewenste duidelijkheid," in *de Architect* 11, no. 3 (March 1980): 48–53.

_____. "Koolhaas ontwerp voor uitbreiding van de Tweede Kamer," in *de Architect* 11, no. 5 (May 1980): 49–63.

_____. "Kwaliteit sluitpost van

goedkoop cultuurbeleid," in *de Architect* 15, no. 4 (April 1984): 24–32.

_____. "Lintas-kantoor te Amsterdam," in *de Architect* 16, no. 7–8 (July–August 1985): 34–37.

_____. "Woning-bouwfestival Den Haag," in *de Architect* 19, no. 4 (April 1988): 66–71.

Photographic credits

The author thanks Rem Koolhaas and his studio, OMA, for kindly providing the illustration materials. Most of the photographs are the work of Hans Werlemann/Hectic Pictures.